Patrice Anne Rutledge

Sams **Teach Yourself**

LinkedIn

in **10 Minutes**

Third Edition

800 East 96th Street, Indianapolis, Indiana 46240

Sams Teach Yourself LinkedIn® in 10 Minutes, Third Edition
Copyright © 2012 by Pearson Education, Inc.

ISBN-13: 978-0-672-33598-3
ISBN-10: 0-672-33598-0
Library of Congress Cataloging-in-Publication data is on file.
Printed in the United States of America
First printing April 2012

Trademarks
All terms mentioned in this book that are known to be trademarks or service marks have been appropriately capitalized. Sams Publishing cannot attest to the accuracy of this information. Use of a term in this book should not be regarded as affecting the validity of any trademark or service mark.

Warning and Disclaimer
Every effort has been made to make this book as complete and as accurate as possible, but no warranty or fitness is implied. The information provided is on an "as is" basis. The author and the publisher shall have neither liability nor responsibility to any person or entity with respect to any loss or damages arising from the information contained in this book or from the use of the CD or programs accompanying it.

Bulk Sales
Sams Publishing offers excellent discounts on this book when ordered in quantity for bulk purchases or special sales. For more information, please contact

U.S. Corporate and Government Sales
1-800-382-3419
corpsales@pearsontechgroup.com

For sales outside of the U.S., please contact

International Sales
international@pearsoned.com

Associate Publisher
Greg Wiegand

Acquisitions Editor
Michelle Newcomb

Development Editor
Charlotte Kughen

Managing Editor
Kristy Hart

Project Editor
Jovana San Nicolas-Shirley

Copy Editor
Mike Henry

Indexer
Erika Millen

Proofreader
Sarah Kearns

Technical Editor
Vince Averello

Publishing Coordinator
Cindy Teeters

Book Designer
Gary Adair

Compositor
Nonie Ratcliff

Contents

About the Author

Patrice-Anne Rutledge is a business technology author and journalist who writes about social media, web-based applications, and small business technology. Her other books include *Sams Teach Yourself Google+ in 10 Minutes*, *Using LinkedIn*, *Using Facebook*, and *The Truth About Profiting from Social Networking*, all from Pearson. Patrice is a long-time LinkedIn member and social networking advocate who has used LinkedIn to develop her business, find clients, recruit staff, and much more. She can be reached through her website at www.patricerutledge.com.

Dedication

To my family, with thanks for their ongoing support and encouragement.

Acknowledgments

Special thanks to Michelle Newcomb, Charlotte Kughen, Vince Averello, Kristy Hart, Mike Henry, and Jovana San Nicolas-Shirley for their feedback, suggestions, and attention to detail.

We Want to Hear from You!

As the reader of this book, *you* are our most important critic and commentator. We value your opinion and want to know what we're doing right, what we could do better, what areas you'd like to see us publish in, and any other words of wisdom you're willing to pass our way.

You can email or write me directly to let me know what you did or didn't like about this book—as well as what we can do to make our books stronger.

Please note that I cannot help you with technical problems related to the topic of this book, and that due to the high volume of mail I receive, I might not be able to reply to every message.

When you write, please be sure to include this book's title and author as well as your name and phone or email address. I will carefully review your comments and share them with the author and editors who worked on the book.

Email: feedback@samspublishing.com

Mail: Greg Wiegand
           Editor-in-Chief
           Sams Publishing
           800 East 96th Street
           Indianapolis, IN 46240 USA

Reader Services

Visit our website and register this book at www.informit.com/title/ 9780672335983 for convenient access to any updates, downloads, or errata that might be available for this book.

Introduction

Although professionals have always acknowledged the value of networking, today's economic climate makes developing a solid network even more critical. LinkedIn, the leading social networking site for professionals, is the ideal tool for maximizing the potential of an online network. LinkedIn has more than 150 million members worldwide, including executives from all Fortune 500 firms and President Barack Obama. Two new members join approximately every second.

It's clear that today's technology has forever changed the way people find a job, promote their businesses, foster strategic partnerships, and develop their professional networks. But technology is just the enabler. The fundamental concepts of professional networking remain the same both online and off. Building relationships through mutual connections and trust is the foundation of success on LinkedIn just as it is in the real world.

Sams Teach Yourself LinkedIn in 10 Minutes, Third Edition is designed to get you up and running on LinkedIn as quickly as possible. This book focuses on standard LinkedIn functionality. LinkedIn rolls out beta functionality and new features on a regular basis, so the features available to you might vary at any given time. The companion website to this book will help keep you updated on what's new with LinkedIn. For now, turn to Lesson 1, "Introducing LinkedIn," to get started with this powerful networking tool.

Who Is This Book For?

This book is for you if...

▶ You're new to LinkedIn and want to become productive as quickly as possible.

▶ You want to find a job or promote your business online, taking advantage of all that social networking has to offer.

▶ You want to become productive on LinkedIn as quickly as possible and are short on time.

Companion Websites

This book has a companion website online at http://www.patricerutledge.com/books/linkedin.

Additional information is located at www.informit.com/title/9780672335983. Here you can find additional lessons and articles, including information about recruiting job candidates and advertising on LinkedIn.

Conventions Used in This Book

The *Sams Teach Yourself* series has several unique elements that help you as you learn more about LinkedIn. These include:

NOTE
A note presents interesting pieces of information related to the discussion.

TIP
A tip offers advice or teaches an easier way to do something.

CAUTION
A caution advises you about potential problems and helps you steer clear of disaster.

PLAIN ENGLISH
Plain English sidebars provide clear definitions of new, essential terms.

LESSON 1

Introducing LinkedIn

In this lesson, you learn the basics of LinkedIn and develop a strategy for success with this popular social networking site.

Understanding What LinkedIn Can Do for You

LinkedIn (www.linkedin.com) is the world's leading social networking site for business, with profiles of more than 150 million professionals around the world. LinkedIn is also rapidly expanding: Two new members join approximately every second. The site is extremely active with recruiters from recruiting firms as well as from major companies such as Microsoft, eBay, and L'Oréal, which makes it a prime hunting ground for job seekers.

Everyone from top CEOs to President Barack Obama has a LinkedIn profile. If you want to network for business on just one social networking site, LinkedIn is the site to choose.

Creating a professional profile and developing a solid network of connections on LinkedIn can help you meet many goals. For example, participation on LinkedIn can enable you to do the following:

- ▶ Find a job or recruit quality job candidates

- ▶ Develop your business by connecting with clients and partners and promoting yourself as a service provider

- ▶ Brand yourself online with a professional presence that demonstrates your expertise

> NOTE: **LinkedIn History**
> LinkedIn was founded in May 2003 when the five company
> founders invited 350 of their closest business contacts to join. By
> the end of that first year, LinkedIn had reached 81,000 members.

Understanding the Key to Success on LinkedIn

The key to success on LinkedIn is to establish clear goals and ensure that all your actions on the site work to achieve those goals.

For example, if your goal is to find a job on LinkedIn, you want to create a strong profile with keywords that attract recruiters. You also want to develop a solid network of professional contacts in your industry—the type of people who might hire you or who might provide relevant job leads.

On the other hand, if your goal is to find business leads and develop your platform as an expert in your field, you could use a different approach. A strong profile and network are still important, but you might also want to participate in LinkedIn Answers and LinkedIn Groups to promote your expertise among LinkedIn's millions of members.

Before establishing your goals, however, you need to understand the unwritten rules of LinkedIn. LinkedIn's focus is on developing a mutually beneficial online business network. With LinkedIn, you can stay in touch with your existing contacts and connect with other professionals who share your goals and interests. LinkedIn is not the place to amass thousands of "followers," engage in heavy sales tactics, or send spam-like communications. Keeping these rules in mind will help you develop a LinkedIn strategy that generates positive results in your professional career.

> TIP: **Focus on Strategy, Not Filling Out Forms**
> At first glance, LinkedIn appears deceptively simple. Its true power,
> however, comes from employing the strategic best practices of
> online networking, not on your ability to enter your professional
> data in a form.

Understanding LinkedIn Account Types

LinkedIn offers several account types, including a free basic account, three premium accounts suited to business users, three Job Seeker accounts, three accounts for sales professionals, and three Talent Finder accounts suited to recruiters. All accounts offer the ability to create a professional profile, develop a network of contacts, search for jobs and people, receive unlimited InMail and requests for introductions, participate in groups, and participate in LinkedIn Answers.

This lesson covers the LinkedIn free account and accounts suited to business users and sales professionals. See Lesson 9, "Finding a Job," for more information about Job Seeker accounts. See Lesson 16, "Recruiting Job Candidates," for more information about Talent Finder accounts.

PLAIN ENGLISH: **InMail**

An InMail is a private message from a LinkedIn member who is not your connection. Although you can receive InMail free if you indicate that you are open to receiving InMail messages, you cannot send InMail unless you pay for that particular service. InMail is a paid service because messages you send via InMail are far less likely to be confused for spam. Keep in mind, however, that InMail isn't the same as the free messages you are able to exchange with your connections after you have already made a connection.

PLAIN ENGLISH: **Introduction**

A LinkedIn introduction provides a way to reach out to people who are connected to your connections. By requesting an introduction through someone you already know, that person can introduce you to the person you're trying to reach. For example, one of your connections might be connected to a hiring manager at a company you want to work for. Requesting an introduction to this hiring manager is a much better way to find a job than just sending a resume along with hundreds of other people.

See Lesson 6, "Communicating with Other LinkedIn Members," for more information about messages, InMail, and introductions.

Using a LinkedIn Free Account

LinkedIn's free account offers so many powerful features that it should suit the needs of most users. Unless you specifically need a premium feature, try out the free account first before making the decision to upgrade. With a free Basic account, you can request a maximum of five introductions at one time, view 100 results per search, and save a maximum of three searches with weekly email alerts.

> NOTE: **LinkedIn Is a Powerful Search Tool**
> You can perform and save targeted searches for people, jobs, companies, and other LinkedIn content. See Lesson 7, "Searching on LinkedIn," for more information about LinkedIn search capabilities.

Exploring LinkedIn Premium Accounts

Premium accounts offer you the ability to contact more people who aren't connected to you and are ideally suited to people using LinkedIn as a business development tool.

> NOTE: **Learn More About LinkedIn Premium Accounts**
> Click the **Upgrade Your Account** link on the bottom menu to view the Subscription Plans page, which provides detailed information about LinkedIn account plans.

LinkedIn's premium accounts enable you to:

▶ Receive an OpenLink Network membership

▶ Send unlimited OpenLink messages

▶ Access the complete list of who's viewed your profile

▶ View expanded profiles of everyone on LinkedIn, even people outside your network

▶ Perform unlimited one-click reference searches

▶ Receive LinkedIn customer service responses within one business day

---

PLAIN ENGLISH: **OpenLink Network**

The OpenLink Network is a LinkedIn premium feature that enables network members to contact each other without incurring additional fees.

Your choice of the specific premium account that's right for you depends on your needs for InMail, introductions, and searches.

Table 1.1 shows the specific features for each level of LinkedIn premium account.

TABLE 1.1 Premium Account Comparison

Feature	Business	Business Plus	Executive
Monthly Price	$24.95	$49.95	$99.95
InMails	3	10	25
Saved Searches	5 with weekly updates	7 with weekly updates	10 with daily updates
Profile Organizer Folders	5	25	50
Profile Results per Search	300	500	700
Pending Introductions	15	25	35

TIP: **Get a Discount by Signing Up for an Annual Plan**

If you sign up for an annual plan, you receive a substantial discount. When purchased annually, the Business account costs $19.95 per month, the Business Plus account costs $39.95 per month, and the Executive account costs $74.95 per month.

Exploring LinkedIn Sales Professional Accounts

LinkedIn offers three levels of Sales Professional accounts, all designed specifically for the needs of sales professionals who use LinkedIn for prospecting. All LinkedIn sales accounts include Lead Builder, which enables to you create and save prospect lists that integrate with Profile Organizer.

Table 1.2 shows the specific features for each level of LinkedIn Sales Professional account.

TABLE 1.2   Sales Professional Account Comparison

Feature	Sales Basic	Sales Navigator	Sales Navigator Plus
Monthly Price	$19.95	$49.95	$99.95
InMails	None	10	25
Saved Searches	5 with weekly updates	7 with weekly updates	10 with daily updates
Profile Organizer Folders	5	25	50
Profile Results per Search	300	500	700
Pending Introductions	15	25	35

You can sign up for a Sales Professional account on a month-by-month basis or receive a discount by purchasing an annual plan.

Creating a LinkedIn Account

Signing up for a LinkedIn account is a simple, straightforward task. Figure 1.1 shows the welcome screen that greets you the first time you visit LinkedIn (www.linkedin.com).

To create your own LinkedIn account, follow these steps:

1. On the LinkedIn home page, enter your first name, last name, email address, and a password. Be sure to create a strong password.

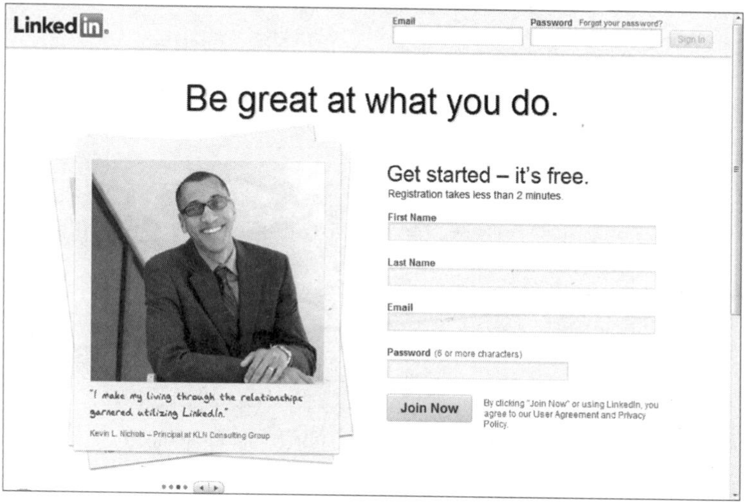

FIGURE 1.1   You can quickly sign up for your own free account from LinkedIn's home page.

A password that contains a combination of uppercase and lowercase letters, numbers, and symbols provides the most protection.

TIP: **Choose the Right Email Address**

LinkedIn offers privacy controls to protect your business email address. Entering the email address that most of your business contacts use to communicate with you yields the best results when others try to connect with you by email on LinkedIn.

---

2. Click the **Join Now** button. The Let's Start Creating Your Professional Profile page appears, shown in Figure 1.2.

3. In the **I Live In** field, select your country. Depending on your choice of country, either the ZIP Code or Postal Code field displays where you can enter the appropriate code. Note that LinkedIn displays only your geographic region, such as San Francisco Bay Area, and not your actual code or city on your profile.

FIGURE 1.2   Enter your basic data to get started on LinkedIn.

4. In the **I Am Currently** field, select your employment status from the options available: Employed, Job Seeker, or Student. The selection you make in this field affects which additional fields display on this page. In this example, we'll use the fields that display if you specify that you're employed. If you select another status, the field you see will differ.

5. Enter your **Job Title**.

6. Enter your **Company**. As you start typing, LinkedIn locates potential company matches from existing profiles. Choosing from an existing entry helps ensure that you and your colleagues are correctly linked by company.

7. If LinkedIn doesn't find an existing match for the company you enter, the **Industry** field appears. Select the industry that best describes your professional expertise from a list of more than 100 options. These options range from popular professions (Accounting, Banking, Computer Software, Internet, Real Estate, and Marketing) to the more obscure (Dairy, Gambling & Casinos, Fishery, and Think Tanks).

8. Click the **Create My Profile** button to open the See Who You Already Know on LinkedIn page.

9. LinkedIn prompts you to search for and connect with people you already know. However, I recommend that you create your profile before completing this step. Why? Because when your contacts receive your connection request, you want them to view a complete profile, not an empty one. To bypass this task for now, click the **Skip This Step** link.

10. Next, LinkedIn prompts you to confirm your email address. What displays on this page varies based on the email provider you use. Complete the verification process based on the prompts LinkedIn provides you.

NOTE: **Understand the Email Verification Process**

As a security measure, LinkedIn needs to verify the email address you entered when you signed up*for an account. This ensures that the person who actually owns an email account, and not an impostor, signed up for LinkedIn.

---

11. LinkedIn prompts you to let your Facebook friends and Twitter followers know that you just joined LinkedIn. Again, I recommend that you click the **Skip This Step** link and inform your social media contacts after you've created your profile.

12. On the Your Account is Set Up—Choose Your Plan Level page (see Figure 1.3), you can choose to start with a free basic account or upgrade immediately to a premium account. Unless you're certain that you need the features offered with a premium account, I suggest that you start with the free account. To do so, click the **Choose Basic** button.

LinkedIn displays your home page (see Figure 1.4), welcoming you to the site.

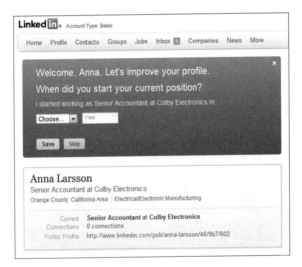

Linked in.

Your Account is Set Up — Choose Your Plan Level

What Do You Want to Do? What's this?	Premium	Basic (Free)
Create a professional profile and build your network	✓	✓
Join industry or alumni groups	✓	✓
Search & apply for jobs	✓	✓
See who's viewed your LinkedIn Profile	✓	Limited
View the professional profiles of over 135 million people	✓	Limited
Send messages to people you aren't directly connected to	✓	
Premium search filters & automated search alerts	✓	
Save profiles into folders	✓	
Add notes & contact info to any profile	✓	
Reach out to over 135 million users	✓	
	Choose Premium	Choose Basic
	Plans starting from $24.95	Free

Skip this step »

FIGURE 1.3   Choose to start with a free Basic account or upgrade immediately to access premium features.

Linked in. Account Type: Basic

Home   Profile   Contacts   Groups   Jobs   Inbox 🔲   Companies   News   More

Welcome, Anna. Let's improve your profile.
When did you start your current position?
I started working as Senior Accountant at Colby Electronics in:

[Choose... ▼] [Year]

[Save] [Skip]

Anna Larsson
Senior Accountant at Colby Electronics
Orange County, California Area | Electrical/Electronic Manufacturing

Current	**Senior Accountant at Colby Electronics**
Connections	0 connections
Public Profile	http://www.linkedin.com/pub/anna-larsson/46/9b7/602

FIGURE 1.4   Your home page is your main LinkedIn dashboard.

TIP: **Stay Logged In to LinkedIn**

Now that you have a LinkedIn account, click the **Sign In** link whenever you visit the site to log on again with your primary email address and password. If you forget your password, click the **Forgot Password?** link on the Sign in to LinkedIn page to request a new one. If you always use the same computer to access LinkedIn, such as a home computer, you can remain logged in for up to 24 hours as a convenience.

Exploring the LinkedIn Home Page

When you first create a LinkedIn account, your home page (refer to Figure 1.4) displays minimal content, which is understandable considering that you don't have any contacts yet. A welcome box greets you, encouraging you to improve your profile.

It's important to remember that the content on your home page is dynamic and is unique to your LinkedIn actions, network, and account settings. After you start participating on LinkedIn, your home page changes. As an active LinkedIn user, the left column of your home page includes the following content:

▶ Your current status and a text box for updating your status. See Lesson 5, "Managing and Updating Your Profile," for more information about updates.

▶ LinkedIn Today headlines, displaying popular articles shared on LinkedIn and Twitter by people in your network. To view more news, select **LinkedIn Today** from the News menu on the global navigation bar at the top of the page.

▶ The latest updates from your network. By default, this section displays all updates, but you can narrow this to display only updates from co-workers, articles people have shared, updates from group members, profile updates, and so forth. You can also search updates by keyword and specify which updates display on your home page. See Lesson 4, "Customizing Your LinkedIn Settings," for more information about customization options.

TIP: **View Your Network Updates as an RSS Feed**

Select **RSS** from the More drop-down list (next to All Updates on your home page) to open the LinkedIn RSS Feeds page where you can subscribe to your LinkedIn network updates and read them in a feed reader. See Lesson 4 for more information on RSS and feeds.

The right column of your home page displays

▶ A list of three people you might know based on your existing connections. You can click the Connect link below a name to send an invitation to connect. If you haven't added any connections yet on LinkedIn, this option won't appear.

▶ A box with advertisements.

▶ The Who's Viewed Your Profile? box, which tells you how many people have viewed your profile recently. To access details about who has viewed your profile, you must either allow others to view your name and headline when you visit their profiles or upgrade to a premium account. If you haven't created a profile yet or no one has viewed your profile, this option won't appear.

▶ The Your LinkedIn Network box. This box lists your number of connections, the total size of your network, and the number of new people in your network.

▶ Boxes for LinkedIn applications and features, such as Events, LinkedIn Answers, Jobs, and Amazon Reading List recommendations. LinkedIn uses the information from your profile to determine relevant content to display. For example, if you select Marketing as your industry, the content displayed should be useful to a marketing professional. See Lesson 13, "Using LinkedIn Applications," to learn more about LinkedIn applications.

> TIP: **Customize the Applications That Appear on Your Home Page**
>
> To remove a box that displays in this column, click the X button in the upper-right corner of the box. Be aware that not every box is available for deletion. To add application boxes, click the **Add an Application** button at the bottom of the column to select from the available options.

Navigating LinkedIn

Navigating LinkedIn is a straightforward process after you understand its navigational structure. LinkedIn pages display two navigation tools: a global navigation bar at the top of the screen and a bottom menu of additional options.

The global navigation bar, shown in Figure 1.5, includes links to the most popular LinkedIn destinations, with drop-down menus offering additional options. Links on the top navigation menu include the following:

- ▶ **Home**—Return to the LinkedIn home page.

- ▶ **Profile**—Edit or view your profile and recommendations.

- ▶ **Contacts**—Manage, add, and import connections.

- ▶ **Groups**—View your groups, view a group directory, or create a group.

- ▶ **Jobs**—Perform an advanced job search or manage job postings.

- ▶ **Inbox**—View, send, and archive LinkedIn messages.

- ▶ **Companies**—View and edit company information.

- ▶ **News**—View LinkedIn Today and your saved articles.

- ▶ **More**—Choose one of the following destinations from the drop-down menu: Answers, Learning Center, Skills, Upgrade Your Account, and Get More Applications. This menu also includes links to your installed applications, such as Events or Reading List by Amazon.

FIGURE 1.5   LinkedIn's global navigation bar provides links to common tasks.

A search box appears to the right of the global navigation bar. See Lesson 7 to learn more about LinkedIn search options.

Above the global navigation bar, in the upper-right corner of your screen, you see a link to your name. Click this link to open the Edit Profile page. Click the down arrow to the left of your name to access a drop-down menu with the following links:

▶ **Settings**—Customize the way you use LinkedIn.

▶ **Sign Out**—Log off LinkedIn.

The Add Connections link displays to the right of your name. Click it to send invitations to potential LinkedIn connections.

The bottom of the LinkedIn screen provides links to additional menu options, including LinkedIn company information, LinkedIn tools, and premium features.

You learn more about these and other LinkedIn features later in this book.

Summary

In this first lesson, you learned about the many features LinkedIn offers, strategies for using the site, how to sign up for an account, and basic navigational tools. Next, it's time to create your profile.

LESSON 2

Creating Your Profile

In this lesson, you learn how to create a LinkedIn profile that generates results.

Viewing a LinkedIn Profile

Profiles form the foundation of LinkedIn. Your profile is your LinkedIn calling card, providing a quick snapshot of your professional background and experience.

Figure 2.1 illustrates a sample LinkedIn profile.

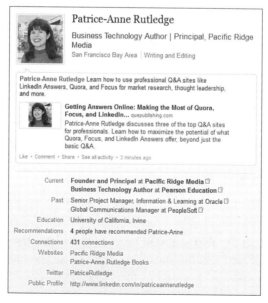

FIGURE 2.1 A solid profile generates positive results on LinkedIn.

A profile can include the following:

- ▶ A summary of your professional experience and specialties

- ▶ Your photo

- ▶ Your current status with comments from your network

- ▶ A list of the positions you've held and your major accomplishments at each

- ▶ A list of the educational institutions you've attended and your major accomplishments at each

- ▶ Sections where you can list certifications, courses, test scores, publications, awards, patents, volunteer experience, languages you speak, and specific skills you have

- ▶ Professional recommendations

- ▶ Data from LinkedIn applications such as your blog feed, Amazon reading list, shared presentations, attached resume, and more

- ▶ A list of your LinkedIn connections

- ▶ Information about your interests, association memberships, honors, and awards

- ▶ Your contact settings

- ▶ A list of your opportunity preferences

Creating a Profile That Achieves Your Goals

Before you create your profile, you need to think strategically about what you want to accomplish. Here are some tips for creating a quality profile:

- ▶ **Set goals for what you want to achieve on LinkedIn**—Are you looking for a job? Do you want to develop your business and find new clients? Are you a recruiter seeking passive job candidates? Make sure that everything you include in your profile works toward achieving that goal.

▶ **Make a list of keywords that relate to your experience, education, certifications, profession, and industry**—Every industry has its buzzwords, and you need to include these if they're terms a recruiter or potential client would search for. For example, an IT professional might include keywords such as Java, Oracle, SAP, or AJAX. A project manager might select PMP, PMI, UML, SDLC, or Six Sigma. A public relations professional, on the other hand, could choose PRSA, APR, or social media.

▶ **Have your current resume handy for easier profile completion**—You can refer to it for any necessary dates or other data you might have forgotten.

CAUTION: **A Profile Isn't a Resume**

Remember, though, that a profile shouldn't duplicate your resume. A profile is a strategic summary of your professional background designed to achieve specific goals.

TIP: **Use the Box.net Files Application to Attach Documents to Your Profile**

If you really do want to include a resume on your LinkedIn profile, consider adding the Box.net Files application. With Box.net, you can share files such as PDF or Word documents on your profile. See Lesson 13, "Using LinkedIn Applications," for more information about Box.net.

▶ **Check for spelling and grammar errors**—Nothing detracts more from a good profile than numerous typos.

▶ **Remember that most people just scan your profile**—You need to capture their attention quickly and not overwhelm them with unnecessary details that detract from your goals.

▶ **Keep it professional**—A few personal details such as your interests help humanize your profile, but too much emphasis on outside activities also detracts from your professional goals.

> CAUTION: **Protect Your Privacy**
>
> Keep privacy issues in mind as you complete your profile. Enter only data that you're willing to share publicly.

Understanding Profile Completeness

To view your own profile, select **Edit Profile** from the Profile drop-down menu on the global navigation bar. The Edit Profile page opens, shown in Figure 2.2.

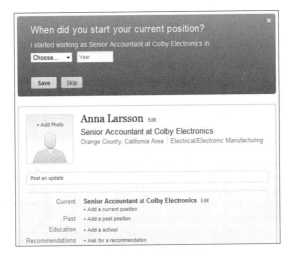

FIGURE 2.2   Create your profile on the Edit Profile page.

On the right side of your screen, you'll see a box that displays your profile completeness. It should be about 25% at this point, just for signing up for a LinkedIn account. This box displays a list of the additional percentage points you receive for completing specific tasks.

To achieve a profile completeness of 100%, you need to complete the following items:

- ▶ Your current position

- ▶ At least two past positions

- ▶ Your education

- ▶ A profile summary

- ▶ A profile photo

- ▶ Your specialties

- ▶ At least three recommendations

Having a complete profile encourages people to network with you. In fact, LinkedIn indicates that users with complete profiles are 40 times more likely to receive opportunities than those with incomplete profiles.

TIP: **Move Beyond What a Computer Thinks Is Complete**

Just filling out the required fields to achieve 100% completion doesn't guarantee success. You also need the right profile content. A few words in a field might count toward a computer's view of "completeness," but it won't be effective if your profile still contains minimal information.

Entering Basic Profile Information

Now that you have a plan for creating a solid profile, it's time to get started entering data. To add more content to the basic profile that LinkedIn creates when you sign up, select **Edit Profile** from the Profile drop-down menu on the global navigation bar.

The Edit Profile page displays your name, title, company, location, and industry based on the data you entered when you signed up. Click the **Edit** link next to your name to open the Basic Information page.

The Basic Information page also includes several new fields. These include:

▶ **Former/Maiden Name**—If you've changed your name at any point during your career, it could be difficult for former classmates or colleagues to find you. Entering your former or maiden name makes it easier when people search for your former name.

▶ **Display Name**—By default, LinkedIn displays your full name. If you have strong privacy concerns, you can choose to display only your first name and last initial to anyone other than your own connections.

▶ **Professional Headline**—LinkedIn uses a combination of your title and company name as your professional headline, which should be sufficient for most people. You might want to customize this, however, if you're seeking work, are self-employed, or maintain more than one job. Some people include targeted keywords, professional certifications, or degrees in their professional headlines.

Some examples:

▶ PMP-certified IT Project Manager Seeking New Opportunities

▶ Bestselling Author, Coach, and Business Consultant

▶ Public Relations Executive, MBA, APR, Fellow PRSA

Make your changes and then click the **Save Changes** button to return to the Edit Profile page.

TIP: **Let the LinkedIn World Know What You're Doing**

The Post an Update link on the Edit Profile page prompts you to share information with your LinkedIn connections. You can enter something now or wait until you have connections who can actually view your updates. See Lesson 5, "Managing and Updating Your Profile," for more information about updates.

Adding Positions

Although you already entered your current job title and company when you created your LinkedIn account, you'll want to expand on that basic information. Click the **Edit** link next to your current position on the Edit Profile page to open the Edit Position page, shown in Figure 2.3.

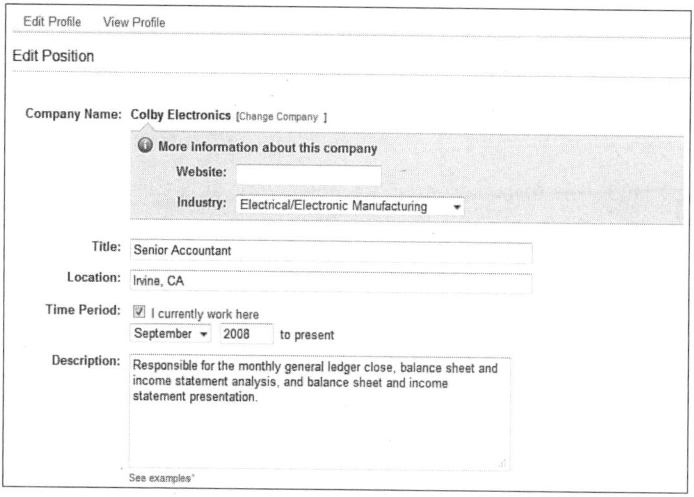

FIGURE 2.3 Let other LinkedIn members know about your professional success.

Enter a brief description of your current position, make any additional changes to the information you previously entered, and click the **Update** button.

Here are a few tips on what to include in the Description field:

▶ **Use keywords**—Think of the terms people would search for and use them in your description. For example, if you work in IT, mention actual technologies rather than vague generalizations.

▶ **Emphasize accomplishments over job duties**—For example, rather than saying that you're responsible for sales, focus on your sales achievements and awards.

▶ **Be brief**—The Description field is a summary, not a detailed resume.

▶ **Keep your goals in mind**—If you want to attract recruiters, think about what would interest them in a potential candidate. If you're seeking clients for your business, focus on what would make them want to hire you.

> NOTE: **Remove Positions You No Longer Want to Appear on Your Profile**
>
> Click the **Remove This Position** link on the Edit Position page to delete that position from LinkedIn.

If you hold more than one current job, click the **Add a Current Position** link on the Edit Profile page to add another current position. This is particularly useful for self-employed or independent professionals who have several income sources. For example, if you're an author, consultant, and blogger, you could choose to combine these activities under one position or create a unique position for each activity.

Add past positions by clicking the **Add a Past Position** link on the Edit Profile page. Adding past positions is important because it provides a clearer view of your background and makes it easier to connect with your former colleagues at previous companies.

> TIP: **Focus on the Last 10 to 15 Years of Employment**
>
> If you have extensive experience, it's a good idea to focus only on the past 10 to 15 years of your work life unless an early position in your career is very relevant to your current goals.

Adding Educational Information

Next, you'll add information about your educational background. LinkedIn uses this information to help you connect easily with former classmates.

Consider the following best practices when choosing what educational information to enter:

- ▶ Include colleges and universities from which you received a degree.

- ▶ Include *relevant* certificates and continuing education coursework. For example, if you're looking for a job in a new field and have completed a related certificate, you should include this information.

▶ Don't include every continuing education course or seminar you've ever taken. It's important to be strategic, not prolific.

▶ Don't include your high school information unless you're still in college, are a recent graduate, or specifically want to reconnect with high school classmates.

To enter educational information, follow these steps:

1. Click the **Add a School** link on the Edit Profile page. The Add Education page opens, shown in Figure 2.4.

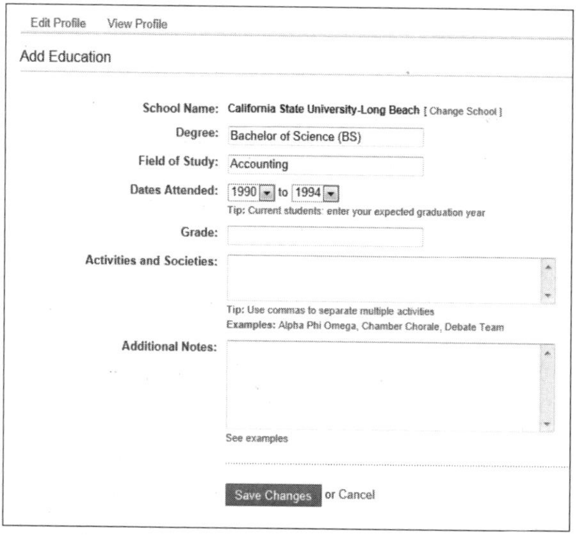

FIGURE 2.4 Provide a summary of your educational accomplishments.

2. Start typing the name of your school in the **School Name** field and then select it from the drop-down list that displays. If you can't find your school in the list, you can enter it manually in the **School Name** field.

3. Enter your degree, such as BA, BS, or MBA.

4. Enter your field(s) of study. This can be your major, an area of concentration, or the name of a certificate.

5. In the Dates Attended fields, enter the years you attended. If you're still a student, enter your anticipated year of graduation in the second field.

NOTE: Deciding Whether to Include Graduation Years

The decision whether to include your year of graduation is a personal choice for many experienced professionals. LinkedIn doesn't require you to list the year you graduated; this is an optional field. Keep in mind, however, that LinkedIn won't be able to automatically search for your former classmates if you omit your graduation year. You would need to perform a manual search for former classmates.

---

6. List relevant activities in the Activities and Societies field. This might include honors, study abroad, and any extracurricular activities. Optionally, enter your GPA (grade point average) in the Grade field.

7. Add any additional notes about your educational experience.

8. Click the **Save Changes** button to return to the Edit Profile page.

NOTE: Enter Only Relevant Information

You don't need to complete all the fields on the Add Education page to provide an accurate picture of your educational background. For example, details about your participation with the ski club or theater groups 20 years ago won't add real value to your LinkedIn profile unless they relate to your current career. Entering the most pertinent data ensures that people who read your profile focus on what's relevant.

The next section on the Edit Profile page, Recommended, encourages you to request professional recommendations. My recommendation, however, is for you to first complete your profile and then add connections before requesting recommendations. See Lesson 10, "Requesting and Providing Recommendations," for more information about LinkedIn recommendations.

Adding Website Links and Other Additional Information

To list websites on your LinkedIn profile—as well as add other information about your interests and achievements—follow these steps:

1. Click the **Add a Website** link on the Edit Profile page. The Additional Information page opens, shown in Figure 2.5.

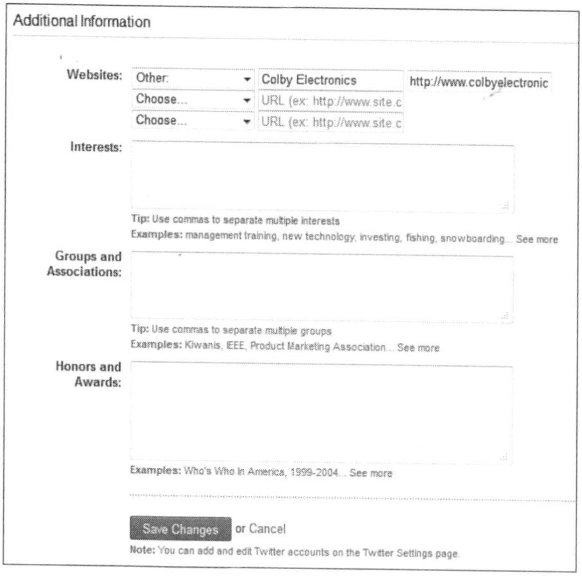

FIGURE 2.5 Add links to your website or blog on your LinkedIn profile.

2. From the Websites drop-down list, select the type of link you want to add. Options include Personal Website, Company Website, Blog, RSS Feed, Portfolio, or Other. If you select Other, a text box appears in which you can enter the name of your choice.

> TIP: **Gain Name Recognition for Your Sites**
>
> You can use the Other option to gain name recognition for your site or blog. For example, if you have a blog called Project Management Best Practices, you might prefer to create a link with that name rather than using the generic "Website" or "Blog." In addition, you can use this field to link to your business's Facebook page or other social sites.

3. Enter the complete URL of the site you want to link to, such as http://www.patricerutledge.com.

> NOTE: **You Can List a Maximum of Three Sites**
>
> To avoid clutter and prevent link spam, you can enter only three websites on your LinkedIn profile. If you have more than three sites to consider, think carefully about which sites would generate the most interest on a business networking site such as LinkedIn.

4. In the Interests text box, enter a list of your professional and personal interests. Be sure to use commas to separate interests so this content is searchable. Each interest becomes a link on your actual profile that you can click to search for others who share your interests. Again, think about meaningful keywords for this section rather than lengthy descriptions.

5. List the groups and associations to which you belong. Use commas to separate this information as well because the terms also become searchable links on your profile.

6. List any honors and awards you've received.

7. Click the **Save Changes** button to update your profile and return to the Edit Profile page.

Integrating Your LinkedIn Account with Twitter

If you have an account on Twitter (www.twitter.com), you might want to consider integrating it with LinkedIn. By doing so, you can share selected Twitter updates.

To set up LinkedIn to integrate with Twitter, follow these steps:

1. On the Edit Profile page, click the **Add a Twitter Account** link.

2. In the dialog box, enter your Twitter username or email as well as your password. If you're already logged in to Twitter, LinkedIn skips this step.

3. Click the **Authorize App** button.

When you add a Twitter account, LinkedIn does the following by default:

▶ Displays your Twitter username on your LinkedIn profile

▶ Shares tweets that contain the #in or #li hashtag on your LinkedIn status

▶ Displays a picture, page title, and short description with a link

If you want to change the default settings, remove a Twitter account, or add another Twitter account, click the **Edit** link to the right of the Twitter field on the Edit Profile page. The Manage Your Twitter Settings dialog box opens (see Figure 2.6), where you can manage how LinkedIn integrates with Twitter. Click the **Save Changes** button when you finish updating the settings in this dialog box.

You can also share your LinkedIn updates on Twitter by selecting the **Twitter** check box when you post updates (see Lesson 5).

FIGURE 2.6   Manage how LinkedIn integrates with Twitter.

Customizing Your Public Profile and URL

LinkedIn makes a public version of your profile available to all web users, regardless of whether they're LinkedIn members or connected to you. When someone searches your name on Google or Yahoo!, for example, the public version of your profile appears in search results. Although a public profile is a great way to promote your career and gain visibility, it isn't for everyone. Don't worry. You have control over exactly what others can view on your profile. You can even hide your profile from public view if you choose.

Customizing Your Public Profile URL

By default, your public LinkedIn URL looks something like this: http://www.linkedin.com/pub/patrice-rutledge/13/521/845. The numbers in this URL address aren't very user-friendly, however, so customize your public profile URL to something easier to remember, such as www.linkedin.com/in/patriceannerutledge, by following these steps:

1. On the Edit Profile page, click the **Edit** link to the right of your Public Profile URL. The Your Public Profile URL and Customize Your Public Profile boxes display on the right side of the Edit Profile page, as shown in Figure 2.7.

Customize Your Public Profile

Control how you appear when people search for you on
Google, Yahoo!, Bing, etc.

Profile Content
○ Make my public profile visible to no one
● Make my public profile visible to everyone
    ☑ Basics
       Name, industry, location, number of recommendations
    ☐ Picture
    ☑ Headline
    ☑ Summary
       └☑ Specialties
    ☐ Current Positions
    ☐ Past Positions
    ☑ Skills
    ☑ Languages
    ☐ Education
    ☐ Additional Information
    ☐ Interested In...

Your public profile URL

Your current URL
http://www.linkedin.com/in/felicemantel
Customize your public profile URL • View your public profile

Profile Badges
Create a profile badge to promote your profile like this:
[View my profile on Linked**in**]

FIGURE 2.7   Create a user-friendly URL for your LinkedIn public profile.

2. In the Your Public Profile URL box, click the **Customize Your Public Profile URL** link.

3. Enter the custom URL you prefer in the Customize Your Public Profile dialog box. Using your first name and last name as one string of characters is a good choice. Spaces, symbols, and special characters aren't allowed in your URL. If someone else is already using the URL you want, LinkedIn lets you know this and offers several available alternatives based on your first and last name.

4. Click the **Set Custom URL** button to save your changes and close the dialog box.

Customizing Your Public Profile

You can specify exactly which fields are visible on your public profile in the Customize Your Public Profile box. Simply clear the check box next to any fields you do not want to appear on your public profile. Click the **View Your Public Profile** link in the Your Public Profile URL box to preview what your public profile looks like on the Web.

> TIP: **You Can Hide Your Profile from Public View**
>
> By default, your public profile is visible to everyone. To hide your entire profile from public view on the Web, click the **Make My Public Profile Visible to No One** option button in the Customize Your Public Profile box.

Adding Profile Sections

LinkedIn enables you to add sections to your profile that share information about your certifications, languages spoken, patents, publications, skills, and other qualifications.

To add a section to your profile, follow these steps:

1. On the Edit Profile page, click the **Add Sections** link. The Add Sections dialog box opens, shown in Figure 2.8.

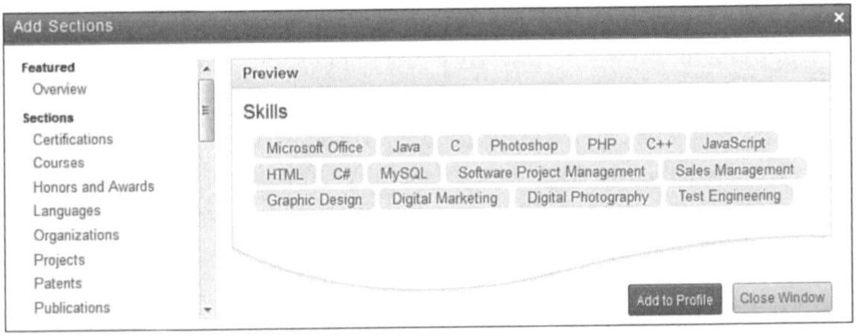

FIGURE 2.8 Add sections to your profile to share more information about your achievements.

2. On the left side of the box, select the type of section you want to add. Choices include Certifications, Courses, Honors and Awards, Languages, Organizations, Projects, Patents, Publications, Skills, Test Scores, and Volunteer Experiences and Causes. In this example, we'll choose Skills, one of the most popular sections to add. Be aware that if you choose another option, the remaining steps will differ.

3. Click the **Add to Profile** button. Depending on your choice in step 3, a new LinkedIn page opens. Because we chose Skills, the Add Skills page opens. Figure 2.9 shows this page.

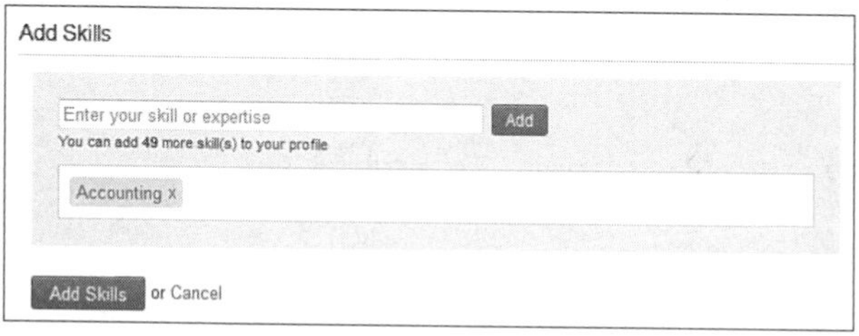

FIGURE 2.9   Let prospective employers and clients know about your skills.

4. Start typing the name of a specific skill and select a match from the drop-down list that displays. Optionally, manually enter a skill that doesn't display in this list and click the **Add** button to add it. For example, if you're a software project manager, you could list Software Project Management as one of your skills.

5. Repeat step 4 to add as many as 50 skills.

6. Optionally, click each skill to open a pop-up box where you can select your proficiency level and years of experience.

7. When you finish adding skills, click the **Add Skills** button to add this section to your profile.

After adding a section to your profile, you can edit or delete this content by clicking the **Edit** link next to the profile section.

Adding a Profile Summary

The next section on the Edit Profile page asks you to enter a profile summary. This is an important step because people scanning your profile often read this section first.

To create your summary, follow these steps:

1. On the Edit Profile page, click the **Add Summary** link to the right of the Summary heading. The Summary page opens, shown in Figure 2.10.

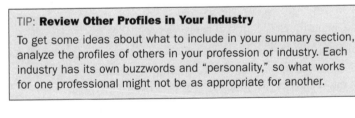

FIGURE 2.10   Provide a concise summary of your professional accomplishments.

TIP: **Review Other Profiles in Your Industry**

To get some ideas about what to include in your summary section, analyze the profiles of others in your profession or industry. Each industry has its own buzzwords and "personality," so what works for one professional might not be as appropriate for another.

---

2. Enter a summary of your professional experience and goals. In addition to summarizing your professional experience, you can also use this field to indicate that you're looking for job opportunities (assuming you're currently unemployed), recruiting staff, accepting new clients, or seeking new business partners, for example. Be sure to keep it professional, however. This is not the place for an advertisement or sales hype.

3. List your specialties in the Specialties field.

4. Click the **Save Changes** button to return to the Edit Profile page.

The next four sections—Experience, Education, Recommendations, and Additional Information—appeared earlier on the Edit Profile page. You can click the **Edit** links in any of these sections to make additional changes, or you can continue to the next section.

Adding Personal Information

Near the bottom of the Edit Profile page, you'll find the Personal Information section. In this section, you can enter the following data: phone, address, IM (instant message), birthday, and marital status.

If you want to add any of this information to your profile, click the **Add** link to open the Personal Information page. The Birthday, Birth Year, and Marital Status fields display a lock button next to them. Select one of the following option buttons to specify your visibility settings: My Connections, My Network (people up to three degrees away from you), or Everyone.

CAUTION: **Consider Your Personal Privacy**

Entering any data in the Personal Information section is optional. Carefully consider your personal privacy before making any personal information public, even to a restricted group of people.

Specifying Contact Settings

Next, specify what types of messages you'll accept and what opportunities you're interested in. To update the Contact Settings page, shown in Figure 2.11, follow these steps:

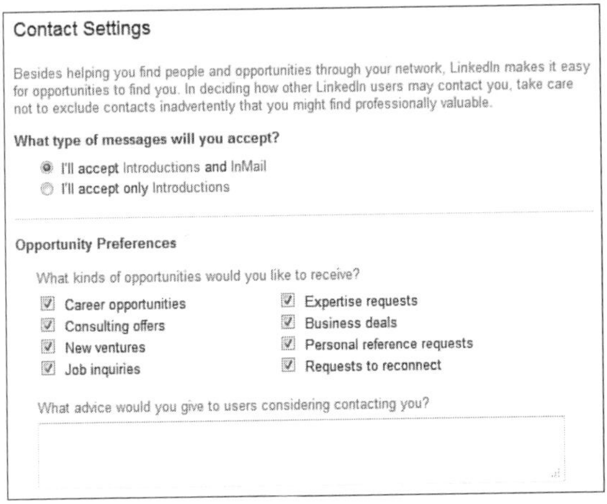

Contact Settings

Besides helping you find people and opportunities through your network, LinkedIn makes it easy for opportunities to find you. In deciding how other LinkedIn users may contact you, take care not to exclude contacts inadvertently that you might find professionally valuable.

What type of messages will you accept?

- ● I'll accept Introductions and InMail
- ○ I'll accept only Introductions

Opportunity Preferences

What kinds of opportunities would you like to receive?

- ☑ Career opportunities
- ☑ Consulting offers
- ☑ New ventures
- ☑ Job inquiries
- ☑ Expertise requests
- ☑ Business deals
- ☑ Personal reference requests
- ☑ Requests to reconnect

What advice would you give to users considering contacting you?

FIGURE 2.11   Tell other LinkedIn members about your contact preferences.

1. At the bottom of the Edit Profile page, click the **Change Contact Preferences** link next to the Contact [First Name] For heading.

2. In the What Type Of Messages Will You Accept? field, indicate whether you'll accept both introductions and InMail or if you'll accept only introductions. See Lesson 6, "Communicating with Other LinkedIn Members," for more information about InMail and introductions. In general, accepting InMail is a good idea if you want people you don't know to be able to contact you, such as recruiters.

3. In the Opportunity Preferences section, indicate the opportunities you're open to. If you're looking for a job or recruiting staff, for example, it's important to let people know this.

4. Enter the advice you would give to members considering contacting you. In this text box, you can indicate that you're open to connecting with new people, you want to connect only with people you know, and so forth.

5. Click the **Save Changes** button to return to the Edit Profile page.

Just below the Contact section on the Edit Profile page is the Applications section, which suggests several applications you can add to your profile. See Lesson 13 for more information about the many ways you can benefit from LinkedIn applications.

Adding a Profile Photo

Finally, you should add a photo to your LinkedIn profile. A photo helps bring your profile to life and sets you apart from other LinkedIn members. A professional headshot works best on your LinkedIn profile.

To upload your photo, follow these steps:

1. At the top of the Edit Profile page, click the **Add Photo** link.

2. Click the **Browse** button, shown in Figure 2.12, to open the Choose File to Upload dialog box. Depending on your browser or operating system, this dialog box could have a different name.

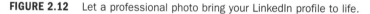

FIGURE 2.12   Let a professional photo bring your LinkedIn profile to life.

3. Select the photo you want to upload and click the **Open** button. Depending on your browser or operating system, the name of this button could vary.

> NOTE: **Photo Format and Size Limits**
> You can upload a photo in a JPG, GIF, or PNG file format. The file cannot be larger than 4MB.

4. Click the **Upload Photo** button. LinkedIn shows you a preview of how your photo will appear on your profile.

5. Use LinkedIn's resizing tool to make any modifications, and click the **Save Photo** button to complete the upload process.

6. Indicate your photo visibility preferences. You can specify that your photo is visible to your connections, to your network, or to everyone. Note that your connections include only the people you directly connect with; your network includes the people connected to your connections.

7. Click the **Save Settings** button to finish the upload and return to the Edit Profile page.

TIP: **Easily Replace or Remove Your Photo**

If you want to replace or remove your profile photo, click the **Edit** link below your photo on the Edit Profile page. Here you can upload a new photo or click the **Delete Photo** link to remove your photo.

Viewing Your Profile

To preview your profile, click the **View Profile** button on the Edit Profile page. Review all your entries carefully, checking for content accuracy as well as for grammar and spelling errors. If necessary, return to the Edit Profile page to revise any of your entries.

See Lesson 5 for information about keeping your profile updated, printing your profile, and promoting your profile on the Web.

NOTE: **You Can Create Profiles in Multiple Languages**

If you speak a language other than English, consider creating a profile in that language as well. To do so, click the **Create Your Profile in Another Language** link on the Edit Profile page (it's just above the profile completeness box on the right side of the page).

Summary

In this lesson, you learned how to create a quality profile that should help you achieve your goals on LinkedIn. Next, it's time to start adding connections.

LESSON 3

Adding and Managing Connections

In this lesson, you learn how to develop a solid LinkedIn connection strategy, connect with other members, and manage your contacts.

Developing a Connection Strategy

After creating a strong profile, the next step in making the most of your LinkedIn experience is developing a solid network of professional connections. Before you add connections to LinkedIn, however, you should develop a connection strategy that matches your goals and networking philosophy.

TIP: **Match Your Connection Strategy with LinkedIn Goals**

In Lesson 1, "Introducing LinkedIn," you established goals for what you want to accomplish on LinkedIn. Be sure that your connection strategy helps you meet these goals. For example, if you're looking for a new job in a specific industry, your focus will be to connect with recruiters and other professionals in that industry. If your LinkedIn goal is to develop your business or build a platform, you might want to connect with a broader spectrum of people.

The three most common approaches are

- ▶ **Connect only with people you know**—LinkedIn members who follow this approach connect only with colleagues, classmates, and associates they personally know or who their known connections recommend to them.

- ▶ **Connect with people you know plus strategic contacts you would like to know**—With this approach, you connect with people you know and also seek out strategic connections who match your networking goals.

- ▶ **Connect with anyone and everyone**—Some LinkedIn members, particularly those who want to use the site for business development purposes, are open networkers, and like to connect with as many people as possible and make special efforts to connect with thousands of people.

PLAIN ENGLISH: **Open Networker**

An *open networker* is a LinkedIn member who is open to connecting with people they don't know. Several LinkedIn groups exist for open networkers, such as LION (LinkedIn Open Networker) and TopLinked. Although it's a good idea to network with new people and develop a mutually beneficial business relationship, be careful not to abuse open networking by connecting indiscriminately just to amass a very large network. Don't treat your LinkedIn network as a numbers game.

Which approach is best? There is no one right answer for everyone. Each LinkedIn member has his or her own goals for what he or she hopes to accomplish on the site as well as his or her own networking strategies and comfort levels.

To get started, consider connecting with current and former colleagues, current and former classmates, friends, and fellow members of professional associations.

Who to connect with beyond these obvious contacts depends on your connection strategy and networking philosophy.

Building Your Network

LinkedIn offers several ways to build your network. You can:

▶ Import your webmail or desktop email contacts and search for them on LinkedIn

▶ Search for current and former colleagues based on the companies listed on your profile

▶ Search for current and former classmates based on the schools listed on your profile

▶ Search for other people you know using LinkedIn's advanced search functionality

▶ Send an invitation request to someone who doesn't use LinkedIn yet

Keep in mind that you don't need to use all these methods to develop your pool of LinkedIn connections. For example, you might not want to connect with all your webmail or address book contacts. Or your webmail account might contain personal email addresses, not the email addresses your contacts used to sign up for LinkedIn.

Importing Webmail Contacts

If you have an email account with a popular webmail provider (such as Gmail, Windows Live Hotmail, Yahoo! Mail, or AOL), LinkedIn can import the email addresses of your web contacts.

To import webmail contacts, follow these steps:

1. Click the **Add Connections** link above the global navigation bar.

TIP: **Alternative Method to Import Webmail Contacts**

You can also import webmail contacts by entering your webmail address and password in the welcome box that displays on your home page.

2. In the See Who You Already Know on LinkedIn box, enter your email and password for the email account whose contacts you want to import.

3. Click the **Continue** button. LinkedIn imports the contacts from your webmail contact list and displays a list of these contacts as shown in Figure 3.1.

FIGURE 3.1   Select the webmail contacts you want to connect with on LinkedIn.

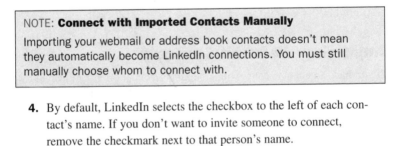

NOTE: **Connect with Imported Contacts Manually**

Importing your webmail or address book contacts doesn't mean they automatically become LinkedIn connections. You must still manually choose whom to connect with.

4. By default, LinkedIn selects the checkbox to the left of each contact's name. If you don't want to invite someone to connect, remove the checkmark next to that person's name.

5. Click the **Add Connection(s)** button to send your invitations. Your contacts will receive your invitations to connect on LinkedIn and choose to accept or reject them.

NOTE: **Confirm Your Email Address Before Connecting**

You can't send invitations to connect until you confirm your email address. If you need to request a new confirmation message from LinkedIn, click the down arrow to the left of your name on the global navigation bar and select **Settings** from the drop-down menu. On the Account & Settings page, click the **Change** link next to the Primary Email field, and then click the **Send Confirmation Email** link to the right of the email address you want to confirm. LinkedIn sends you an email with confirmation instructions. Be aware that the Send Confirmation Email link doesn't display if you've already confirmed your email address.

Importing Contacts from Other Email Systems

Although LinkedIn imports webmail contacts automatically, you need to export your contacts from desktop email systems as a separate step. To do so, follow the instructions your email system provides for exporting your email address book data to one of the following:

- ▶ A comma-separated values file (.CSV), which is a computer file in which fields are separated by commas

- ▶ A vCard file (.VCF) for electronic business cards

- ▶ A tab-separated file (.TXT), which is a computer file in which fields are separated by tabs

LinkedIn accepts the following files for import:

- ▶ CSV files from Microsoft Outlook

- ▶ CSV or tab-separated files from Palm Desktop

- ▶ CSV files from ACT!

- ▶ vCard files from Palm Desktop

- ▶ vCard files from Mac OS X Address Book

To import a file exported from a desktop email system, follow these steps:

1. Click the **Add Connections** link above the global navigation bar.

2. In the See Who You Already Know on LinkedIn box, click the **Import Your Desktop Email Contacts** link.

TIP: **Alternative Navigation to Import Email Contacts**
You can also import email contacts by clicking the **Import Your Desktop Email Contacts** link in the welcome box on your home page.

3. Click the **Browse** button to select the appropriate file on your computer. Depending on your browser or operating system, the name of this dialog box and button might vary.

TIP: **Option for Outlook Users**
If you're importing contacts from Outlook, click the **Import from Outlook** button instead of the Browse button.

4. In the Choose File to Upload dialog box, select the file you want to upload and click the **Open** button. Depending on your browser or operating system, the name of this dialog box and button might vary.

5. Click the **Upload File** button. LinkedIn imports the contacts from your webmail contact list and displays a list of these contacts (refer to Figure 3.1).

NOTE: **Resolving File Upload Problems**
If there is a problem with your upload, LinkedIn displays an error message and doesn't complete the import process. The most common reason for receiving an error message is that you tried to upload a file that isn't in one of the supported formats.

6. Select the check box to the left of each contact's name you want to invite to connect on LinkedIn. Be aware that importing your contacts doesn't mean they automatically become LinkedIn connections. You must still manually choose whom to connect with.

7. Click the **Add Connection(s)** button to send your invitations.

Connecting with Current or Past Colleagues

To connect with current or past colleagues, follow these steps:

1. Click the **Add Connections** link above the global navigation bar.

2. Click the **Colleagues** tab, shown in Figure 3.2.

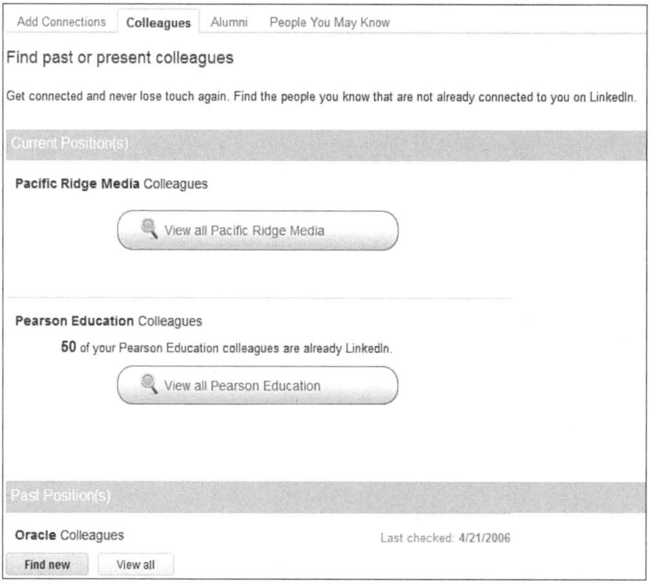

| Add Connections | **Colleagues** | Alumni | People You May Know |

Find past or present colleagues

Get connected and never lose touch again. Find the people you know that are not already connected to you on LinkedIn.

Current Position(s)

Pacific Ridge Media Colleagues

View all Pacific Ridge Media

Pearson Education Colleagues

50 of your Pearson Education colleagues are already LinkedIn.

View all Pearson Education

Past Position(s)

Oracle Colleagues   Last checked: 4/21/2006

Find new   View all

FIGURE 3.2 Connecting with your current and past colleagues is a great way to build your online network.

3. Based on the current and past positions you entered on your profile, LinkedIn displays related company names and buttons that help you locate potential matches. Click the button that best matches the search you want LinkedIn to perform.

4. From the list of potential matches, select the individuals you know and want to connect with by placing a check box before their names.

5. Click the **Send Invitations** button to send invitations to these people.

TIP: **Personalize Your Invitation**

Select the **Add a Personal Note with Your Invitation?** check box to add a personalized greeting to your invitation to connect. Personalizing your request is particularly useful when reaching out to colleagues you haven't worked with in a while.

Connecting with Former Classmates

To connect with current or former classmates, follow these steps:

1. Click the **Add Connections** link above the global navigation bar.

2. Click the **Alumni** tab.

3. Click the button for the university you want to search from the list of schools from your profile.

TIP: **Search for Former Classmates from All the Schools You Attended**

If you didn't finish adding schools to your profile, click the **Add Another School to Your Profile** link to find classmates from additional schools.

---

4. On the Alumni page (see Figure 3.3), you can narrow search results by dates attended, workplace, profession, and location.

5. Review the alumni listed at the bottom of the page and click the **Connect** link to send an invitation to the people you recognize.

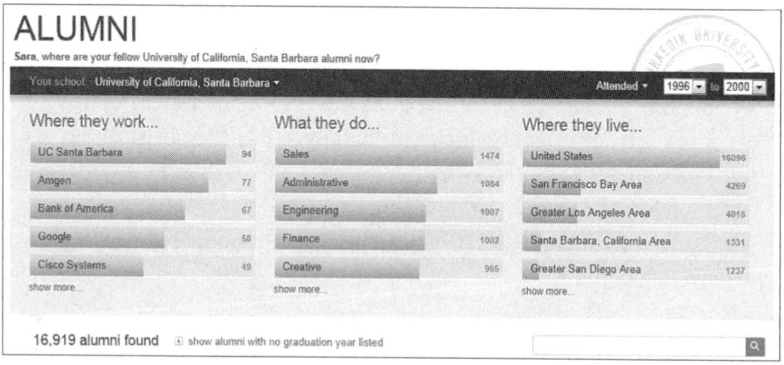

FIGURE 3.3   Search for former classmates on the Alumni page.

Connecting with Other LinkedIn Members

By now, you should have a good start on developing your LinkedIn network. Here are a few other suggestions for finding worthwhile connections on LinkedIn:

- ▶ **Review the list of people your connections are connected to, which displays in their profile**—It's very likely that you know some of the same people and would like to connect with them as well. View the profile of the person you want to connect with and click the **Add [First Name] to Your Network** link to send an invitation. For example, to connect with Anne Smith, you would click the **Add Anne to Your Network** link.

- ▶ **Search for individuals by name in the Search People box on the top navigation menu**—Click the **Add to Network** link to the right of the person you want to connect with to create and send an invitation.

- ▶ **Search by keyword and location to find local members of your professional associations**—Click the **Advanced** link on the top navigation menu to access the Advanced People Search page. For example, you could search for the keyword PRSA (for the Public Relations Society of America) and the postal code

92606 within a 25-mile radius to find fellow PRSA members in Orange County, California.

▶ **Search for potential connections among the members of any LinkedIn groups to which you belong**—The Members tab provides a list of all group members with a link to their profiles. Remember, however, not to spam fellow group members with connection invitations. Be selective in determining who you want to connect with.

See Lesson 7, "Searching on LinkedIn," for more information on searching for people.

When you click the **Add to Network** link from any of these options, a page prompting you to create an invitation appears, shown in Figure 3.4.

FIGURE 3.4   Specify how you know a target connection before sending an invitation.

To create an invitation on this page, follow these steps:

1. Select how you know your target connection from these options:

▶ **Colleague**—Select a company from the drop-down list that appears.

- ▶ **Classmate**—Select a school from the drop-down list that appears.

- ▶ **We've Done Business Together**—Select a company from the drop-down list that appears.

- ▶ **Friend**

- ▶ **Groups**—Select a LinkedIn group from the drop-down list that appears.

- ▶ **Other**—Enter the person's email address.

- ▶ **I Don't Know [First Name]**

2. Include a personal note in the text box explaining why you want to connect on LinkedIn. This is particularly important if you don't know the person you want to connect with.

3. Click the **Send Invitation** button to send your invitation to connect.

See Lesson 6, "Communicating with Other LinkedIn Members," for more information on viewing the status of connection invitations and other messages.

> **TIP: Consider Other Options for Contacting People You Don't Know**
>
> Two other ways of connecting with people you don't know are to send an InMail or request an introduction. See Lesson 6 for more information on InMail and introductions.

Connecting with People Not on LinkedIn

If you discover that some of your real-world networking contacts aren't using LinkedIn yet, it's easy to invite them:

1. Click the **Add Connections** link above the global navigation bar to open the Add Connections page.

2. In the Enter Email Address box (see Figure 3.5), enter the email address of the person or persons you want to invite. Separate multiple addresses with a comma.

Enter Email Addresses

Enter email addresses of people to invite and connect. Separate each address by a comma.

anna.larsson949@gmail.com

Send Invitations

FIGURE 3.5   Invite your real-world connections to join LinkedIn.

3. Click the **Send Invitations** button to send invitations.

Responding to Connection Invitations

In addition to sending invitations to connect, you might also receive invitations. To respond to an invitation, follow these steps:

1. Click the **Inbox** link on the global navigation bar to open your inbox. If you have new messages, LinkedIn displays the number of messages in parentheses, such as Inbox (2).

2. Click the **Invitations** tab to view your open invitations, shown in Figure 3.6. Alternatively, you can also view new invitation requests in your inbox preview on your home page.

NOTE: **Receive Invitations to Connect by Email**

If you specified that you want to receive invitations to connect by email on the Account & Settings page, your invitations also arrive by email. Click the link in the email to open the Invitations page.

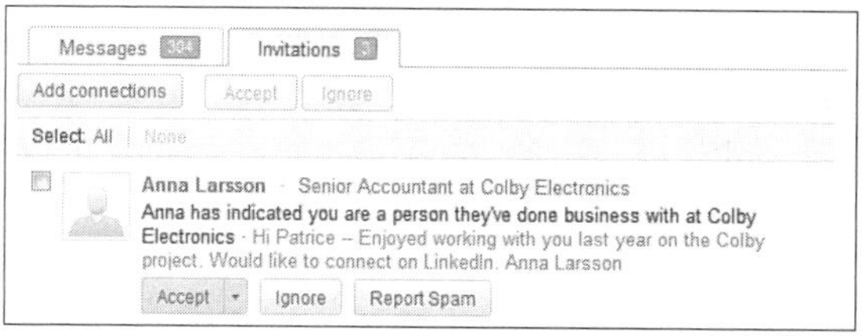

FIGURE 3.6   See who wants to connect with you on the Invitations tab.

3. If you would like to view the profile of a person who wants to connect, click the sender's name. Reviewing a LinkedIn member's profile can help you remember more about someone you don't know well or decide whether to connect with someone you don't know at all.

4. Take one of the following actions:

    ▶ If you want to add the person to your network, click the **Accept** button.

    ▶ If you want to send a message to the person who initiated the invitation before accepting or declining, click the down arrow to the right of the Accept button and select **Reply** from the menu. For example, you might want to ask why this person wants to connect before accepting.

    ▶ If you don't want to accept this invitation, click the **Ignore** button. LinkedIn moves this invitation to your Archived folder where you can view and respond to this invitation at a later time. After ignoring an invitation, LinkedIn provides two additional options: the I Don't Know [First Name] link and the Report as Spam link. Clicking the **I Don't Know** link blocks this person from inviting you again and alerts LinkedIn that this was an unwanted invitation request. Clicking the **Report as Spam** link reports the sender to LinkedIn.

    ▶ Click the **Report Spam** button to report the sender to LinkedIn. You can report an invitation as spam even if you don't ignore it.

CAUTION: **Think Carefully Before Clicking the I Don't Know or Report as Spam Links**

Because LinkedIn can penalize other users for sending too many requests to people they don't know—or for sending spam—think carefully before choosing these options. Selecting one of these options is too harsh if it's a genuine request from someone you just don't want to connect with.

When you accept invitations, LinkedIn adds those members as 1st degree connections in your network. You can add notes about the person and edit their contact information in the Contact Information section on the right side of their profile.

Managing Your Connections

After you develop your LinkedIn network, you need an easy way to find and manage your existing connections. The Connections page offers several ways to do this.

Click the **Contacts** link on the global navigation bar to open the Connections page, which displays a list of your connections (see Figure 3.7).

Select a connection to display more information on the right side of the screen. Here you can click a name to open this person's profile, click the **Send Message** link to send a message on LinkedIn, edit details such as IM username or birthday, view an email address and work information, or enter tags that identify how you know this person. Clicking the **Edit Tags** link enables you to apply any of the following tags to a connection: classmates, colleagues, friends, group members, or partners.

If you have many connections, it might be difficult to find the person you're looking for. LinkedIn offers several ways to filter your connections. You can

▶ Hover your mouse over the ABC link to select a letter of the alphabet. LinkedIn displays only connections with a last name starting with that letter.

▶ Enter a keyword in the search box and then click the **Search** button.

▶ Narrow your results by tag, company, location, industry, or recent activity.

FIGURE 3.7   Find, contact, and manage your connections on the Connections page.

Removing Connections

If you decide that you no longer want to connect with someone on LinkedIn, you can remove that person as a connection:

1. Click the **Contacts** link on the global navigation bar to open the Connections page.

2. Click the **Remove Connections** link in the upper-right corner of the page.

3. Select the check box next to the connections you want to remove.

4. Click the **Remove Connections** button.

People you remove are no longer able to view any data that can be viewed only by actual connections, and they also can't send you direct messages.

LinkedIn, however, doesn't notify them of the fact they have been removed.

CAUTION: **Remove Connections for the Right Reason**

Be sure that a connection really warrants removal before proceeding with the removal process. For example, if a connection you don't know well is bothering you with requests, spam, or sales pitches, this person is probably a connection worth removing. Removing former colleagues or associates simply because you haven't seen them in a while or don't work with them anymore can be shortsighted.

Viewing Your Network Statistics

The Network Statistics page provides some interesting statistics about your network, including your total number of connections, the number of members you can reach through an introduction, the number of new people in your network, and much more. To view these stats, select **Network Statistics** from the Contacts drop-down menu on the global navigation bar.

Summary

In this lesson, you learned how to develop a connection strategy that suits your goals and started developing your own network. Next, it's time to customize your LinkedIn settings to give you the optimal online networking experience.

LESSON 4

Customizing Your LinkedIn Settings

In this lesson, you learn how to customize your LinkedIn profile, email, account, and privacy settings.

Customizing the Way You Use LinkedIn

Now that you've created a profile and connected with other LinkedIn members, it's time to customize your LinkedIn settings to optimize your experience on the site.

> TIP: **Customize for Optimal Privacy and Simplicity**
>
> If you're not sure which options to choose, select the ones that provide you the most privacy and simplicity while still enabling you to achieve your goals.

The Account & Settings page provides a lengthy list of options for customizing your LinkedIn experience. To access this page, go to the global navigation bar, click the down arrow to the left of your name, and select **Settings** from the drop-down menu to open the Account & Settings page (see Figure 4.1).

> CAUTION: **Don't Skip Account Customization**
>
> The many options provided on the Account & Settings page might seem overwhelming at first, and you might be tempted to skip this step. Setting aside some time to customize the options on this

page, often a one-time task, can pay off in the long run. By customizing your LinkedIn settings, you'll better protect your privacy,
receive only the specific information you want, and avoid any
unpleasant surprises regarding the way LinkedIn handles your personal data.

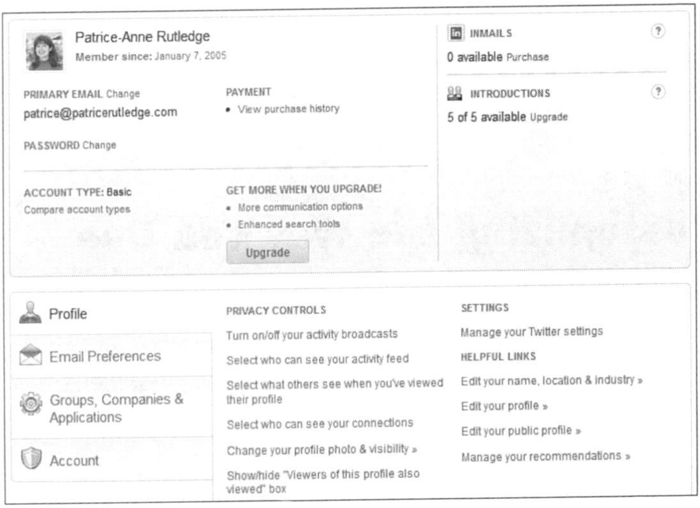

FIGURE 4.1   The Account & Settings page provides numerous options for customizing your LinkedIn experience.

The top portion of the Account & Settings page enables you to do the following:

▶ **Change your email address**—Click the **Change** link next to the Primary Email field to add, change, or delete email addresses. You can also specify your primary email address to which LinkedIn sends all messages.

TIP: **Add All Your Email Accounts to the Email Addresses Page**
Enter all the email addresses you use on the Email Addresses page. This includes your work email, personal email, and school email if you're a recent graduate or still use a university email

account. When people invite you to connect, LinkedIn matches the email address they enter for you to your LinkedIn account. Entering all your email accounts helps ensure a match.

▶ **Change your password**—Click the **Change** link next to the Password field to specify a new password for your account. Changing passwords on occasion is a good security measure. Also, remember to create a strong password that includes a combination of uppercase and lowercase letters, numbers, and symbols.

▶ **View your purchase history**—Click the **View Purchase History** link to view a list of your LinkedIn purchases, such as premium accounts.

▶ **Compare account types**—Click the **Compare Account Types** link to learn about LinkedIn premium accounts. Refer to Lesson 1, "Introducing LinkedIn," to learn more about LinkedIn account options and upgrades.

▶ **Upgrade your account**—Click the **Upgrade** button to upgrade to a premium account.

▶ **Purchase additional InMails**—Click the **Purchase** link next to the InMails field to purchase additional InMails at $10 each. The number of InMails you currently have available displays in this field.

▶ **Purchase additional introductions**—Click the **Upgrade** link next to the Introductions fields to upgrade to a premium account that offers additional introductions. The number of introductions you currently have available displays in this field. Free LinkedIn accounts provide up to five introductions at any one time.

Customizing Profile Settings

To customize your profile settings, go to the global navigation bar, click the down arrow to the left of your name, and select **Settings** from the drop-down menu. By default, the Profile tab is selected on the Account & Settings page (refer to Figure 4.1).

This tab includes the following links:

▶ **Turn on/off your activity broadcasts**—When you update your
  status, modify your profile, or make recommendations, LinkedIn
  broadcasts this activity on the home page of your connections.
  For most people, this provides good exposure on the LinkedIn
  network. If you want to block these notifications, however, you
  can turn them off.

▶ **Select who can see your activity feed**—Make your activity feed,
  which displays in the right column of your profile, visible to
  everyone on LinkedIn or restrict it to only your network or your
  connections. For maximum privacy, you can choose not to display your activity feed.

PLAIN ENGLISH: **Your Connections Versus Your Network**

Your Connections refers to the LinkedIn members you connect with
directly. *Your Network* refers to the people two or three degrees
away from your connections (in other words, your connections' connections). See Lesson 6, "Communicating with Other LinkedIn
Members," for more information on this distinction.

▶ **Select what others see when you've viewed their profile**—
  Customize what, if anything, LinkedIn publishes about you when
  you visit a LinkedIn member's profile. Options include displaying your name and headline, anonymous profile characteristics
  (such as industry and title), or nothing at all. If you're using
  LinkedIn as a business development tool, you might want others
  to know that you visited their profile. Otherwise, you might prefer complete or partial anonymity.

NOTE: **Choosing to Remain Anonymous Affects Profile
View Stats**

Be aware that you must allow LinkedIn to display your name and
headline to see who's viewed your own profile with a free account.
If you want to remain anonymous, you must upgrade to a premium
account to gain access to this information.

▶ **Select who can see your connections**—By default, LinkedIn allows your direct connections to browse a list of your other connections. This can provide a useful way to develop your network because it's quite likely that you might know some of your connections' connections. If you want to hide your connections list, however, you can choose to do so. Your connections can still view shared connections, however.

▶ **Change your profile photo & visibility**—Upload or remove your profile photo. If you don't want everyone to view your photo, you can restrict its visibility to only your network or only your connections. Refer to Lesson 2, "Creating Your Profile," for more information and uploading and editing profile photos.

▶ **Show/hide "Viewers of this profile also viewed" box**—Specify whether you want other LinkedIn members to see this box on the right column of your profile. It helps people find other LinkedIn members to connect with, but can also lead people to your competitors.

▶ **Manage your Twitter settings**—Enable your LinkedIn account to integrate with Twitter. If you've already added your Twitter account, you can change your access settings or disable the integration at any time. Refer to Lesson 2 for more information about integrating LinkedIn and Twitter.

▶ **Edit your name, location & industry**—Open the Basic Information page where you can edit your name, headline, location, and industry. Additionally, specify the display name you want others to see. If you have strong privacy concerns, you can choose to display only your first name and last initial (such as Patrice R.) to people who aren't your connections. Displaying your full name will yield better search results, however.

▶ **Edit your profile**—Update and edit your profile content on the Edit Profile page. Refer to Lesson 2 for more information about this page.

▶ **Edit your public profile**—Specify the content you want to include in your public profile and customize your web URL. Refer to Lesson 2 for more information about editing your public profile.

▶ **Manage your recommendations**—Request, provide, and manage recommendations. See Lesson 10, "Requesting and Providing Recommendations," for more information about the power of LinkedIn recommendations.

Customizing Email Notification Settings

LinkedIn enables you to customize the way you handle email notification of various actions and activities. To customize your email notification settings, click the down arrow to the left of your name on the global navigation bar, select **Settings** from the drop-down menu, and select the **Email Preferences** tab on the Account & Settings page (see Figure 4.2).

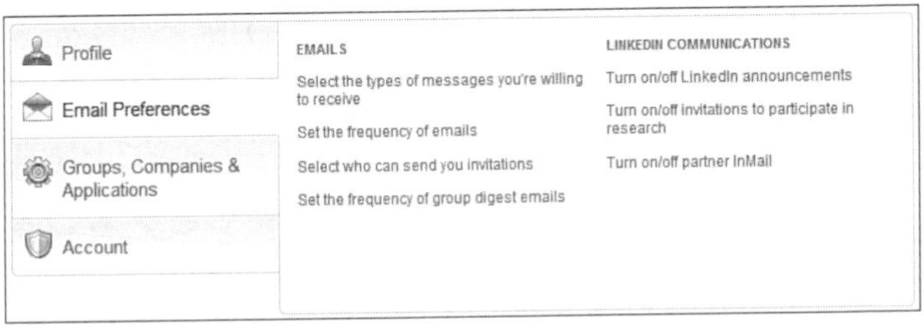

	EMAILS	LINKEDIN COMMUNICATIONS
Profile	Select the types of messages you're willing to receive	Turn on/off LinkedIn announcements
Email Preferences	Set the frequency of emails	Turn on/off invitations to participate in research
Groups, Companies & Applications	Select who can send you invitations	Turn on/off partner InMail
Account	Set the frequency of group digest emails	

FIGURE 4.2   Customize when and how you receive LinkedIn email notifications.

This tab includes the following links:

▶ **Select the types of messages you're willing to receive**—Specify your contact settings, such as whether you're open to receiving InMail and introductions. Refer to Lesson 2 for more information about specifying your contact settings.

▶ **Set the frequency of emails**—Specify your email frequency
preferences on the Frequency of Email dialog box, shown in
Figure 4.3, for different types of LinkedIn communication such
as invitations, job notifications, network activity, and so forth.
Frequency options include the following:

> ▶ **Individual Email**—LinkedIn sends an email to your pri-
> mary email address as soon as the action takes place.

> ▶ **Weekly Digest Email**—LinkedIn sends one bundled email
> notification per week. With bundled notifications, you
> don't receive a notification if there is no activity.

> ▶ **No Email**—LinkedIn sends no email. You need to go to
> the LinkedIn website to read messages and notifications.

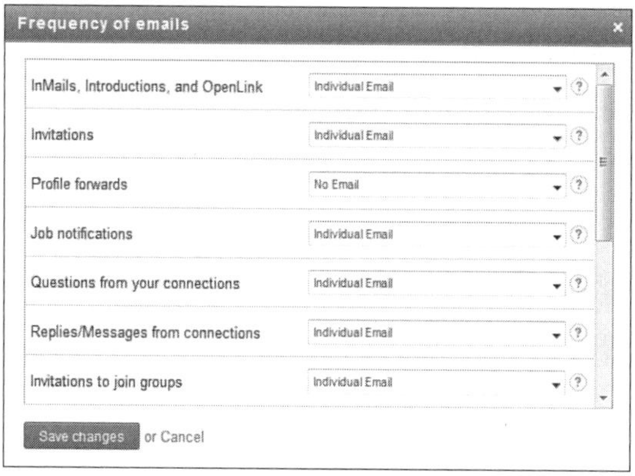

FIGURE 4.3 LinkedIn enables you to provide specific instructions on its
delivery of email messages.

NOTE: **Consider Carefully How to Best Manage Your LinkedIn
Messages**

Many people choose to receive email notifications of the updates
that are most important to them and review online those that are
less time-sensitive. For example, you might want to receive invitations and job notifications immediately, but review group news only
on the Web. If you decide that your choices aren't working well for
you, you can always modify these selections.

▶ **Select who can send you invitations**—By default, you receive all invitations, but you can choose to receive invitations from only those who know your email address or those who are in your Imported Contacts list (such as people who are your contacts in Gmail or Outlook). Keep in mind, however, that restricting your invitations could block an invitation from someone you might actually want to connect with.

▶ **Set the frequency of group digest emails**—For each group you've joined, specify whether you want to receive a weekly digest email, a daily digest email, or no email notification.

▶ **Turn on/off LinkedIn announcements**—Specify whether you want to receive notification of new LinkedIn features and services.

▶ **Turn on/off invitations to participate in research**—Specify whether you want to receive invitations to participate in LinkedIn online market research surveys.

▶ **Turn on/off partner InMail**—Specify whether you want to receive InMail from LinkedIn's marketing or hiring partners.

Managing Group, Company, and Application Settings

You can also customize your settings for groups, LinkedIn Company Pages, and applications. To do so, click the down arrow to the left of your name on the global navigation bar, select **Settings** from the drop-down menu, and select the **Groups, Companies & Applications** tab on the Account & Settings page (see Figure 4.4).

This tab includes the following links:

▶ **Select your group display order**—Specify which groups display on the global navigation bar and in which order. See Lesson 11, "Participating in LinkedIn Groups," for more information on creating and using LinkedIn groups, including how to order and display them.

Profile	GROUPS	APPLICATIONS
Email Preferences	Select your group display order »	View your applications »
	View your groups »	Add applications »
Groups, Companies & Applications	Set the frequency of group digest emails	PRIVACY CONTROLS
	Turn on/off group invitations	Turn on/off data sharing with 3rd party applications
Account	COMPANIES	
	View companies you're following »	Manage settings for LinkedIn plugins on third-party sites

FIGURE 4.4 Manage your group, company, and application settings.

▶ **View your groups**—View a list of the LinkedIn groups you joined.

▶ **Set the frequency of group digest emails**—For each group you've joined, specify whether you want to receive a weekly digest email, a daily digest email, or no email notification.

▶ **Turn on/off group invitations**—By default, you will receive group invitations from your connections. If you don't want to receive these invitations, you can block them.

▶ **View companies you're following**—View a list of the companies you're following, specify your notification settings for each company, and stop following selected companies.

▶ **View your applications**—Open the Authorized Applications page, which enables you to view and remove LinkedIn applications you installed. You can also remove access for external websites that you previously allowed to access your LinkedIn data, such as Business Exchange or InMaps.

▶ **Add applications**—Open the Applications page where you can add, modify, and remove LinkedIn application. See Lesson 13, "Using LinkedIn Applications," for more information.

▶ **Turn on/off data sharing with 3rd party applications**—Specify whether you want to allow LinkedIn to share your data with third-party applications.

▶ **Manage settings for LinkedIn plugins on third-party sites**—Specify whether you want to notify LinkedIn when you visit an external website that uses LinkedIn plugins.

Managing Your Account Settings

The Account Settings tab on the Account & Settings page enables you to manage privacy controls, upgrade your account, subscribe to LinkedIn content via RSS, and other modify other settings.

To access this tab, click the down arrow to the left of your name on the global navigation bar, select **Settings** from the drop-down menu, and select the **Account** tab on the Account & Settings page (see Figure 4.5).

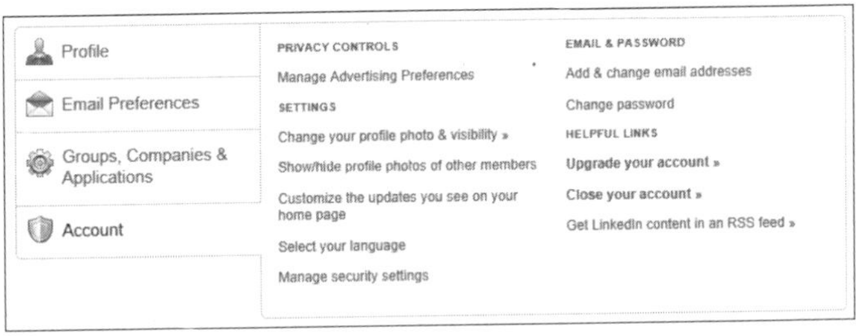

FIGURE 4.5   The Account tab enables you to manage your privacy on LinkedIn.

The Account tab includes the following links:

▶ **Manage Advertising Preferences**—Specify whether you want LinkedIn to show you ads while you're visiting third-party sites while logged into LinkedIn. For more information about LinkedIn advertising preferences, click the **Read More** link in the Manage Advertising References dialog box.

TIP: **Read LinkedIn's Privacy Policy**
To learn more about LinkedIn's privacy policy, click the **Privacy Policy** link on LinkedIn's bottom navigation menu.

▶ **Change your profile photo & visibility**—Upload or remove your profile photo. If you don't want everyone to view your photo, you can restrict its visibility to only your network or only your connections. Refer to Lesson 2 for more information and uploading and editing profile photos.

▶ **Show/hide profile photos of other members**—Choose whose photos you want to view. Options include everyone's photo, no photos, or only photos of people in your network or people who are your connections.

▶ **Customize the updates you see on your home page**—Network updates on your home page give you a quick snapshot of your connections' activities on LinkedIn. Although it's good to keep up with the latest news in your network, you might find that some network updates are of more interest to you than others are. Fortunately, there's a way to customize exactly what appears on your home page. On the Updates You See on Your Home Page dialog box, shown in Figure 4.6, you can specify how many updates you want to view on your home page. The default is 15, but you can choose from 10 to 25 updates. You can also specify the exact updates you want to display by selecting the check box to the left of each update type.

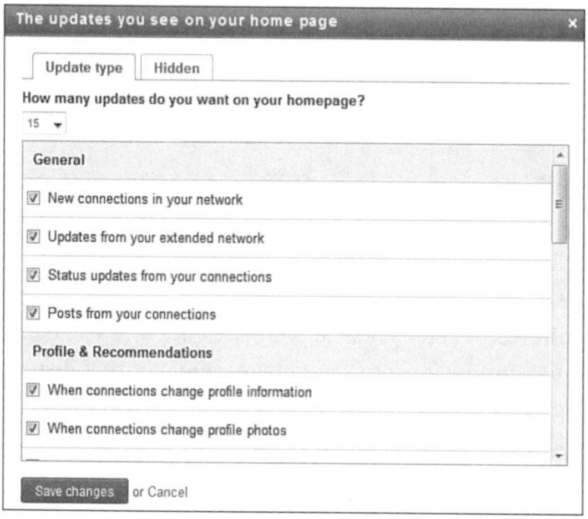

FIGURE 4.6   Customize the content that appears on your home page.

▶ **Select your language**—Select the language in which you want to view the LinkedIn interface. LinkedIn is available in more than a dozen languages.

▶ **Manage Security Settings**—Specify whether you want to use a secure connection (https) when you're browsing LinkedIn. If you're not familiar with secure connections and how they work, click the **Learn More** link in the Security Settings dialog box. Be aware that selecting this setting can affect your access to external LinkedIn applications.

▶ **Add & change email addresses**—Add, change, or delete email addresses. You can also specify your primary email address where LinkedIn sends all messages.

▶ **Change password**—Specify a new password for your account. Changing passwords on occasion is a good security measure. Also, remember to create a strong password that includes a combination of uppercase and lowercase letters, numbers, and symbols.

▶ **Upgrade your account**—Upgrade to a LinkedIn premium account.

▶ **Close your account**—Close your account and specify your reason for doing so. Keep in mind that if you choose this option, you'll lose all your LinkedIn connections and will no longer have access to the site.

▶ **Get LinkedIn content in an RSS feed**—If you use a feed reader such as My Yahoo!, Google Reader, Newsgator, or Netvibes to subscribe to and read your favorite blog and news feeds, you might be interested in adding several LinkedIn feeds. On the LinkedIn RSS Feeds page, shown in Figure 4.7, you can subscribe to a private feed of the network updates that displays on your home page or a public feed of your favorite LinkedIn Answers categories.

PLAIN ENGLISH: **RSS**

RSS stands for *Really Simple Syndication*, a popular format for web feeds. Content publishers can syndicate their content with a feed, making it available for users to subscribe to it and view with feed reader applications. The standard feed icon is a small orange square with white radio waves, letting you know that the content is available via feed for your subscription.

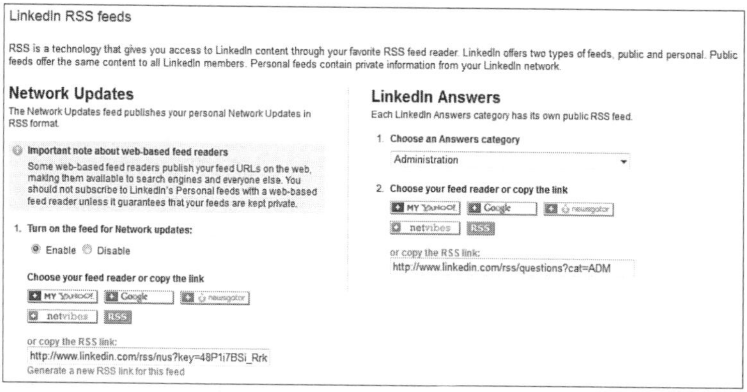

FIGURE 4.7   You can view LinkedIn content with your favorite feed reader.

CAUTION: **Ensuring Feed Privacy**

It's important to understand the difference between a private feed and a public feed. LinkedIn private feeds contain personal data such as your updates and your connections' updates and are meant for your private viewing. Public feeds contain data available for public viewing on the Web, such as the content in LinkedIn Answers. Be careful not to publish your private feed on the Web. If you use a web-based feed reader, verify that your data will remain private if you don't want others to view your LinkedIn network updates.

Summary

In this lesson, you learned how to customize your LinkedIn settings for optimal efficiency and privacy. This often one-time effort will pay off by giving you a much easier, more streamlined system for using LinkedIn. In the next lesson, you learn how to manage and update your profile.

LESSON 5

Managing and Updating Your Profile

In this lesson, you learn how to update your LinkedIn status and profile, promote your profile on the Web, and print and download your profile.

Understanding the Importance of a Current Profile

Keeping your profile current is critical to your success on LinkedIn. Creating your initial profile might be a one-time task, but you need to update it regularly to let others know you're an active participant on LinkedIn. In addition to updating your actual profile, LinkedIn enables you to post frequent updates to inform your network about your activities and accomplishments.

LinkedIn enables you to share important news with other LinkedIn members in text updates of up to 600 characters. You can also insert URLs in your updates with a title, description, and optional photo. For example, you could link to your website, a blog post, or an article on an external news site.

If you want to share your LinkedIn updates on Twitter, you should limit them to 140 characters. Otherwise, only the first 140 characters of your update will display on Twitter. Refer to Lesson 2, "Creating Your Profile," for more information about integrating LinkedIn with Twitter. Figure 5.1 shows an example of a brief text-only update that's suitable for cross-posting on Twitter.

Figure 5.2 shows an example of an update that includes a link to a blog post.

> Sara Wretstrom Just received my certificate in Social Media Marketing from
> the University of California, Irvine.
> Like · Comment · See all activity · 1 minute ago

FIGURE 5.1 Quickly let your connections know what's new in your
professional life.

FIGURE 5.2 Showcase relevant blog posts with a LinkedIn update.

When you post an update, it displays in several places:

- ▶ At the top of your profile just below your name and headline

- ▶ In the Activity section of your profile, located in the right column

- ▶ At the top of your home page

- ▶ On your connections' home page

NOTE: Your Updates Won't Display If You Chose to Hide Them

If you choose to turn off your activity broadcasts or to hide your
activity feed on the Account & Settings page, your updates won't
be visible. Refer to Lesson 4, "Customizing Your LinkedIn Settings,"
for more information about changing these settings.

Your update remains indefinitely until you either delete it or replace it with
a new update.

Although updates are a fun way to let your connections know what's new
in your life, they are also a strategic networking tool. Keep your goals in
mind and post updates that help achieve them. A well-crafted update can
be an effective marketing and publicity tool, but be careful to avoid overt
sales pitches in your updates. An update is a conversation with your network, not an advertisement.

Posting an Update

To post an update on LinkedIn, follow these steps:

1. On the global navigation bar, click the **Home** link to navigate to your LinkedIn home page.

2. Type your update in the Share an Update box that appears at the top of your home page (see Figure 5.3). Remember that you can enter up to 600 characters unless you want to share your update on Twitter. In that case, you should limit your update to 140 characters (Twitter cuts off anything in excess of this length).

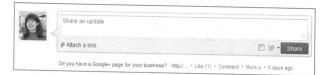

FIGURE 5.3   Post an update to let other LinkedIn members know what you're doing.

NOTE: **Alternative Method for Posting Updates**

Optionally, you can also post an update on the Edit Profile page. To do so, go to the global navigation bar and select **Edit Profile** from the Profile drop-down menu.

---

3. If you want to refer to an external URL, click the **Attach a Link** link. If not, skip to step 9.

4. Enter the URL you want to include in the Add URL box, such as http://www.quepublishing.com.

5. Click the **Attach** button. LinkedIn searches for this URL and displays a title, description, and photo from the content it finds on this page (see Figure 5.4).

6. Optionally, click the **Edit** link to make changes to this default content, described in steps 7 and 8.

7. Enter any changes to the title or description in the text boxes.

FIGURE 5.4   Attach links to relevant external sites, such as websites, blogs, or news sites.

8. The Include Photo check box is selected by default, but you can remove this check mark if you don't want to include a photo. To change from the default photo, click the arrows below the photo to view alternative selections. LinkedIn searches for any photos on the page you're sharing and offers them as options.

9. Click the down arrow to the right of the Visible To drop-down list to specify who can see this update. You can share with everyone on LinkedIn or only with your connections.

10. If you set up LinkedIn to integrate with Twitter, you can select the check box to the left of the **Twitter** icon to share your update on Twitter. If you haven't set up LinkedIn–Twitter integration yet, you're prompted to do so before continuing. Refer to Lesson 2 for more information about setting up this integration.

11. Click the **Share** button to post your update, as shown in Figure 5.5.

FIGURE 5.5   An update as it displays on your profile.

LinkedIn displays this update on your profile and home page. Your connections can also view this update on your profile and on their home pages. If you choose to share with everyone, any LinkedIn member who visits your profile can view your updates, but your updates won't appear on their home pages unless you connect with them.

Managing Your Updates

After posting an update, you can

▶ Delete the update by clicking the **Delete Your Update** button (a large X) in the upper-right corner of your update box on the Edit Profile page or in the [First Name's] Activity section in the right column on this page. After confirming you want to delete this update, LinkedIn deletes it permanently.

▶ Show support for your own update by clicking its **Like** link (although this is usually considered unnecessary).

▶ View a list of your latest updates by clicking the **See All Activity** link below your update. This option is available only on the Edit Profile page, not on your home page.

Understanding How Your Network Can Respond to Your Update

When your update appears on your connections' home page, they can

▶ Show their support for your update by clicking the **Like** link.

▶ Add a comment by clicking the **Comment** link below your update. If your connections have entered comments about your update, you'll see a link beneath your posted update on your home page and on your profile. The link tells you how many comments you have (for example, 2 Comments). Click this link to view your comments and add your own feedback to the discussion.

▶ Send you a private message by clicking the **Send a Message** link.

▶ Share your update with their connections or fellow group members or in an update of their own by clicking the **Share** link. Figure 5.6 shows the Share dialog box, which opens.

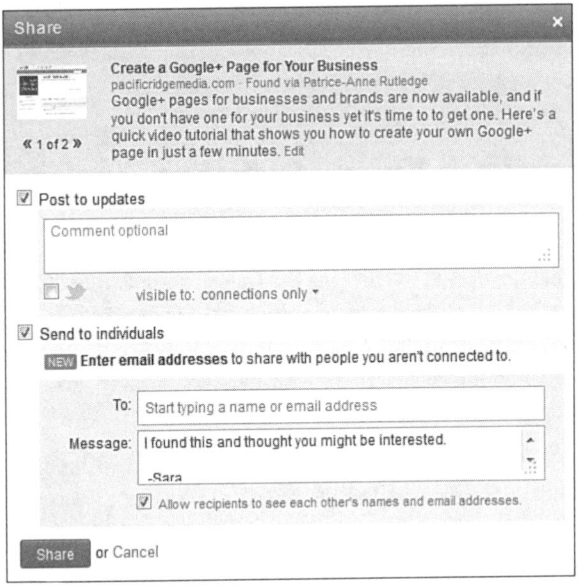

FIGURE 5.6 Share your update with group members and individual connections.

TIP: **Add Comments to Participate in the LinkedIn Community**

Adding your own comments to your connections' updates is a good way to stay in touch and maintain visibility.

Updating Your Profile

Even if you create a thorough profile when you first sign up for LinkedIn, you'll eventually want to update it with recent information.

You should update your LinkedIn profile whenever your employment status changes, you receive a degree or certification, win an award, learn a new skill, start a new business, achieve a career milestone, or change your LinkedIn goals. To update your profile, select **Edit Profile** from the Profile drop-down menu on the global navigation bar. The Edit Profile page opens (see Figure 5.7).

FIGURE 5.7 Be sure to update your profile regularly with new information.

The Edit Profile page is where you first created your profile, so you should already be familiar with its content. After you first enter profile data, links such as Add a Past Position or Add a School disappear. Instead, click the **Edit** link next to any field you want to update. The appropriate LinkedIn page opens, where you can make any required changes.

Refer to Lesson 2 for more information about the content you can enter on the Edit Profile page.

> **CAUTION: Don't Let Your Profile Get Outdated**
>
> Although it's not necessary to update your profile every week, you shouldn't let it get outdated either. If it's obvious that you haven't touched your profile in months, or years, LinkedIn members might not bother contacting you for what could have been a lucrative opportunity for you.

Promoting Your Profile on the Web

With your permission, LinkedIn makes a public version of your profile available for view and search on the Web. Figure 5.8 shows a sample LinkedIn profile link in Google search results.

Patrice-Anne Rutledge | LinkedIn
www.linkedin.com/in/patriceannerutledge
San Francisco Bay Area - Business Technology Author | Principal, Pacific Ridge Media
View **Patrice-Anne Rutledge's** professional profile on **LinkedIn**. **LinkedIn** is the
world's largest business network, helping professionals like Patrice-Anne ...

FIGURE 5.8   Your LinkedIn public profile appears in Google search results.

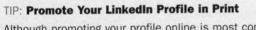

TIP: **Promote Your LinkedIn Profile in Print**

Although promoting your profile online is most common, many LinkedIn members also print their LinkedIn profile URL on business cards, brochures, and other marketing materials.

To customize the appearance of your public profile, click the **Edit** link next to the Public Profile field on the Edit Profile page. Lesson 2 provided details on how to manage your public profile. As a reminder, here are tips to maximize your profile's online visibility:

▶ Customize your public profile URL to make it user-friendly, such as http://www.linkedin.com/in/patriceannerutledge.

▶ Make your public profile visible to everyone in the Customize Your Public Profile box and place a check mark next to all fields you want to appear on your public profile.

▶ Preview your public profile to ensure that you like how it appears to others on the Web.

In addition to maintaining a public profile, you can also post a LinkedIn button on your website, blog, or online resume. Figure 5.9 shows a sample button.

Promote your profile by adding a badge to your blog, online resume, or website:

Choose a button:	... then copy and paste the code (includes a link to your public profile):
View my profile on **Linked** [in] See how we're connected	**TypePad Users** Click here to add this button to your TypePad blog: Add to My TypePad Blog

View my
profile on **Linked** [in]
(160x33)
	`<a href="http://www.linkedin.com/in/patriceannerutledge">`
	`<img src="http://www.linkedin.com/img/webpromo`
	`/btn_viewmy_160x33.png" width="160" height="33" border="0" alt="View`

my **Linked** [in] profile
(160x33)
	`<a href="http://www.linkedin.com/in/patriceannerutledge">`
	`<img src="http://www.linkedin.com/img/webpromo`
	`/btn_myprofile_160x33.png" width="160" height="33" border="0"`

FIGURE 5.9   Add a LinkedIn button to your website so that site visitors can view your profile.

Click the **Create a Profile Badge** link in the Your Public Profile URL box to open the My Profile: Promote page, where you can select the button style you prefer. For example, a blog sidebar is a great place for a LinkedIn button. Copy the HTML code LinkedIn provides and paste it into your own site.

Another way to promote your LinkedIn profile on the Web is to include a link to your public profile URL in your email signature, on your online business card, or on other social sites such as Facebook or Twitter.

Printing and Downloading Your Profile

You can print and download your profile, or the profile of another LinkedIn member, by clicking one of the links that display at the bottom of a member's profile box, as shown in Figure 5.10.

FIGURE 5.10   Print or download your profile using one of the icons.

Your options include:

- ▶ **Share**—Opens a message that enables you to share this profile with another LinkedIn member.

- ▶ **PDF**—Creates a PDF document from your profile that you can view with Adobe Reader (http://get.adobe.com/reader).

- ▶ **Print**—Opens the Print dialog box in which you can specify print options and print a profile.

- ▶ **vCard**—Downloads your profile in the vCard format, which is a file format used for electronic business cards. This option appears only for your own profile or for your connections.

- ▶ **Flag**—Notifies LinkedIn that this profile violates its terms and conditions. For example, you could flag a profile that contains profanity, hate speech, or spam.

Summary

In this lesson, you learned how to update your status and profile, promote your profile on the Web, and print and download your profile. Next, learn the many ways to communicate with other members and become part of the LinkedIn community.

LESSON 6

Communicating with Other LinkedIn Members

In this lesson, you learn about the LinkedIn network and the many ways to communicate with other LinkedIn members.

Understanding Your LinkedIn Network

Before you start communicating with others on LinkedIn, you need to understand how LinkedIn classifies its members in terms of their connections to you. This distinction is important because it determines what, if any, restrictions LinkedIn places on your ability to contact people.

Your LinkedIn network consists of three levels of connections:

► **1st degree connections**—LinkedIn members you connect with directly. Either you sent them an invitation to connect and they accepted, or you accepted their invitations. Your connection list on your profile displays your 1st degree connections. When LinkedIn refers to "your connections," this means your 1st degree connections.

► **2nd degree connections**—LinkedIn members who connect directly with your 1st degree connections.

► **3rd degree connections**—LinkedIn members who connect directly with your 2nd degree connections.

For example, if you connect directly with your colleague Nicole, she is your 1st degree connection. If Nicole connects directly to Ben, her former classmate, Ben is your 2nd degree connection. If Ben connects directly with Drake, one of his co-workers, Drake is your 3rd degree connection.

LinkedIn also considers fellow members of groups as part of your network. See Lesson 11, "Participating in LinkedIn Groups," for more information about LinkedIn groups.

PLAIN ENGLISH: **My Network**

Your LinkedIn network (termed *My Network*) differs from the entire LinkedIn network, which consists of all LinkedIn members. At the time of this printing, the entire LinkedIn network includes more than 135 million members.

TIP: **View Your Network Statistics**

To view how many people are in each level of your network, select **Network Statistics** from the Contacts drop-down menu on the global navigation bar.

Understanding InMail, Introductions, and LinkedIn Messages

LinkedIn offers several ways to communicate with other members. The type of communication you can send depends on how you're connected to these members. Your choices include

▶ **Messages**—Messages are the primary form of communication on LinkedIn. You can send messages to your direct connections as well as to the people who belong to the same LinkedIn groups as you do. If you can send a message to someone, the Send Message link appears next to this person's name on their profile and in search results. See "Sending Messages" later in this lesson for more information. Although you'll often see the term *message* used generically to refer to all items in your inbox, it is a specific type of communication in itself.

▶ **Invitations**—An invitation is a request to connect with another LinkedIn member. Refer to Lesson 3, "Adding and Managing Connections," for more information about sending invitations.

▶ **InMail**—An InMail is a private message to or from a LinkedIn member who is not your connection. You can receive InMail free if you indicate that you are open to receiving InMail messages on the Account & Settings page. In general, sending InMail is a paid LinkedIn feature unless the recipient is a premium member who belongs to the OpenLink Network. See "Sending InMail" later in this lesson for more information.

▶ **Introductions**—An introduction provides a way to reach out to the people who are connected to your connections. By requesting an introduction through someone you already know, that person can introduce you to the person you're trying to reach. You can contact your 1st degree connections to request introductions to members who are 2nd and 3rd degree connections. Members with free accounts can have up to five introductions open at a time. See "Requesting Introductions" later in this lesson for more information.

Understanding Your Contact Options

Before you start communicating with another LinkedIn member, you need to understand your available options for contacting that particular person. When you view member profiles or their summary information from another part of the site, the icons to the right of a member's name tell you how you're connected (see Figure 6.1).

FIGURE 6.1   The icons next to a member's name tell you how you're connected.

These icons identify 1st, 2nd, and 3rd degree connections; LinkedIn premium account holders, and LinkedIn OpenLink network members. If you aren't familiar with a particular icon, hover your mouse over it for a text description.

NOTE: **Some LinkedIn Members Have No Icons**

Members who display no icons next to their names are out of your network and aren't premium account holders.

The buttons and links that display to the right of a member's name let you know what contact options are available. These include

▶ **Connect**—Invite this person to connect on LinkedIn. Refer to Lesson 3 for more information about sending connection requests.

▶ **Send [First Name] a Message**—Send a message to a direct connection or group member.

▶ **Send InMail**—Send an InMail to someone who isn't a direct connection. This option doesn't appear for members to whom you can send a message because it wouldn't make sense to pay to contact someone you can communicate with freely. If you click the **Send InMail** link and don't have a premium account, LinkedIn prompts you to sign up for one before you can proceed.

▶ **Send InMail (Free)**—Send an OpenLink message to a member of the OpenLink Network. LinkedIn members who hold premium accounts can offer you the option of sending them free InMail. Refer to Lesson 1, "Introducing LinkedIn," for more information about the OpenLink Network.

▶ **Recommend [First Name]**—Post a recommendation for this LinkedIn member.

▶ **Get Introduced Through a Connection**—Request an introduction to this member through a 1st degree connection.

▶ **Suggest a Profile Update for [First Name]**—Send profile update suggestions to one of your connections. Although most people want to improve their LinkedIn profiles, be careful to avoid making suggestions that sound like criticisms.

▶ **Suggest Connections**—Suggest other LinkedIn members that this person should consider connecting with.

▶ **Find References**—Search for LinkedIn members who worked at the same company at the same time as this member.

▶ **Save [First Name]'s Profile**—Save this person's profile to your Profile Organizer (a premium feature). See Lesson 7, "Searching on LinkedIn," for more information.

These are the link names that appear on an actual profile. The link names in search results are sometimes abbreviated.

CAUTION: **Not All Options Are Available for All Members**

Remember that you'll never see all these options for any one member. For example, it wouldn't make sense to send InMail, request an introduction, or add to your network a member who is already your connection, so these options don't appear for your connections.

Managing Your Inbox

Your inbox is the focal point for all your direct communication on LinkedIn. Click the **Inbox** link on the global navigation bar to open the Inbox page, shown in Figure 6.2.

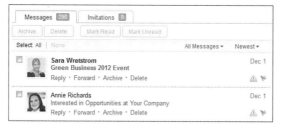

FIGURE 6.2   Your inbox is the focal point for your personal communications on LinkedIn.

TIP: **Preview Your Inbox Without Opening It**
Pause your mouse over the **Inbox** link to preview your three most recent messages.

The default view of your inbox is the Messages tab, which displays all the messages you've received. If you have a lot of inbox messages and want to filter what you see, click the **All Messages** link and choose one of the available options from the drop-down menu. For example, you can choose to display only unread messages, flagged messages, InMails, recommendations, introductions, profiles, jobs, or blocked messages. By default, LinkedIn displays your messages in order from newest to oldest. To reverse this order, click the **Newest** link and select **Oldest** from the drop-down menu.

TIP: **Search for Specific Content**
In addition to filtering inbox items, you can also search for a specific message. Enter a keyword in the Search Inbox box on the left side of the page and click the **Search** button (the button with the magnifying glass). LinkedIn displays all messages containing that search term. For example, you could search for a person's name or a word or phrase in the subject line or message text.

From the Messages tab, you can

▶ View a pop-up box with information about the sender by pausing your mouse over the sender's name. In this box, you can click the **View Profile** link or sender's name to view a complete profile or click the **Download vCard** link to download this person's electronic business card.

▶ View a message by clicking its subject line.

▶ Reply to a message by clicking the **Reply** link below the message's subject line. See "Reading and Replying to Messages" later in this lesson for more information.

▶ Forward a message to another LinkedIn member by clicking the **Forward** link below the message's subject line.

▶ Archive a message by clicking the **Archive** link below the message's subject line. This moves your message to the Archived folder, which you can access at any time by clicking the **Archived** link on the left side of your Inbox. It's a good idea to archive old or resolved messages to keep your Inbox focused on your current action items.

▶ Delete a message by clicking the **Delete** link below the message's subject line. This removes the message from your Inbox and places it in your Trash folder. You can access the Trash folder by clicking the **Trash** link on the left side of your inbox. In this folder, you can choose to empty your trash, undelete a message you deleted by mistake, or delete messages permanently.

TIP: **You Can Archive or Delete Multiple Messages**

To archive or delete more than one message at a time, select the check box to the left of all the messages you want to move and then click either the **Archive** or **Delete** button at the top of the inbox.

▶ Mark a message as read or unread. By default, new messages appear in bold text to signify they have not yet been read. After you read a message, the message no longer is boldfaced in your inbox. To change this, select the check box to the left of a message and click the **Mark Unread** button.

▶ Flag a message as an action item for follow-up. Click the **Flag** icon, which serves as a toggle, to flag or unflag a message for action.

▶ Report a message as spam. Click the **Report Spam** icon (a triangle with an exclamation mark) to notify LinkedIn of a spam message.

The inbox also includes another tab: Invitations. This tab displays all open invitations you need to respond to. Refer to Lesson 3 for more information about responding to invitations to connect.

Sending Messages

To send a message to a 1st degree connection or group member, follow
these steps:

1. On the global navigation bar, select **Compose Message** from the
   Inbox drop-down menu. You can also send a message by clicking
   the **Compose Message** button from your inbox.

2. In the To field, start typing the name of your connection and wait
   for LinkedIn to find a match (see Figure 6.3).

FIGURE 6.3   Sending a direct message to one of your LinkedIn connections.

TIP: **Send a Message to Multiple Connections**

Alternatively, click the address book icon to open your connection
list. With the address book, you can search for the person you
want to reach or select multiple recipients for your message.
LinkedIn enables you to send a message to up to 50 connections
at one time.

---

3. Enter a subject for your message.

4. Enter your message in the text box.

5. If you're sending a message to multiple recipients and don't want to disclose this information, remove the check mark before the **Allow Recipients to See Each Other's Names and Email Addresses** check box (selected by default).

6. To email yourself a copy of your message, select the **Send Me a Copy** check box. Your message already appears in your Sent folder by default.

7. Click the **Send Message** button. LinkedIn sends your message to the recipient and notifies you that your message was sent.

Although clicking the **Compose Message** link is the primary way to send messages on LinkedIn, you can also send messages by clicking **the Send [First Name] a Message** link in a profile, on your home page, or in search results.

TIP: **Other Ways to Contact LinkedIn Members**

The profiles of your direct connections also display their external email address in the Contact Information box on the right sidebar. Some members include their email addresses directly on their profiles for the entire LinkedIn network to see.

Reading and Replying to Messages

In your inbox, click the subject line link of any message to open it. Figure 6.4 illustrates a sample message.

The buttons that appear at the bottom of a message vary depending on the message type and what actions you can take. For example, a basic message includes the Reply button and a recommendation request includes the Write a Recommendation button.

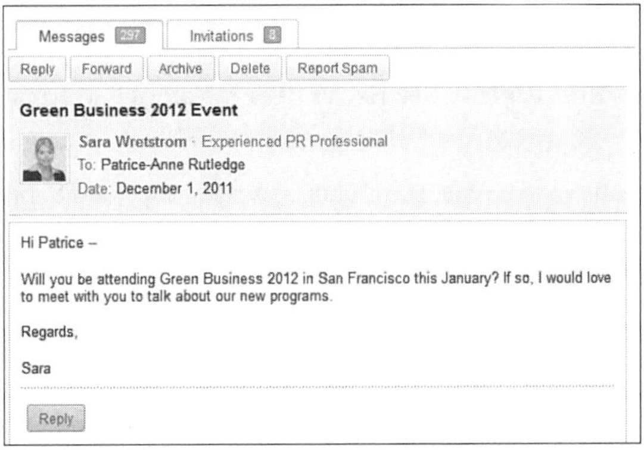

FIGURE 6.4   View a message and reply to it.

Sending InMail

As you learned earlier in this lesson, InMail enables you to contact LinkedIn members who aren't in your network. In an effort to manage spam, LinkedIn requires members to pay to send InMail. InMail is most useful for members who want to contact a wide variety of people, such as recruiters or individuals using LinkedIn for business development.

LinkedIn premium accounts, including Job Seeker premium accounts, enable you to send a fixed number of InMail messages per month. To learn more about LinkedIn premium accounts and InMail, click the **Upgrade Your Account** link on the bottom navigation menu. To learn more about Job Seeker premium accounts, select **Job Seeker Premium** from the Jobs drop-down menu on the global navigation bar.

You can also purchase individual InMails at $10 each. To do so, go to the global navigation bar, click the down arrow to the left of your name, and select **Settings** from the drop-down menu. Then click the **Purchase** link to the right of the InMails field on the Account & Settings page. This is cost-efficient only if you want to contact just a few people by InMail.

Refer to Lesson 1 to learn more about the OpenLink Network and premium account options. See Lesson 9, "Finding a Job," to learn more about
Job Seeker premium accounts.

To determine the InMail options available for a particular member, view
the contact options on that person's profile (see Figure 6.5).

Send InMail Free
Get introduced through a connection
Save Abby's Profile

FIGURE 6.5   Determine the InMail options for a particular LinkedIn member.

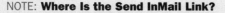

To send InMail to a LinkedIn member, follow these steps:

1. Click the **Send InMail** link on the profile of the person you want
    to reach. If you're sending paid InMail, the Compose Your
    Message page opens. If you're sending free InMail, the Compose
    Your OpenLink Message page opens (see Figure 6.6). These
    pages contain identical information.

2. If you don't want to share your contact information with the per-
    son you want to reach, remove the check mark from the **Include
    My Contact Information** check box (selected by default). In

general, it's a good idea to share contact information. To do so, enter your email address and phone number in the specified fields.

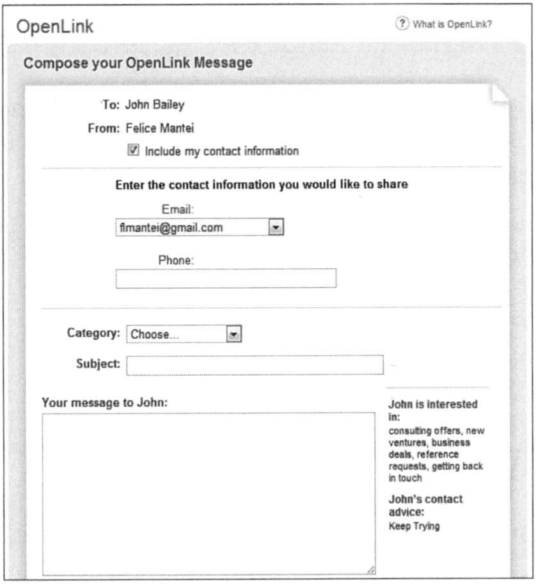

FIGURE 6.6   Sending free InMail to members of the OpenLink Network.

3. In the Category drop-down list, select the reason for your InMail. Options include career opportunity, consulting offer, new venture, job inquiry, expertise request, business deal, reference request, or get back in touch.

4. In the Subject field, enter the subject of your InMail.

5. In the text box, enter your message. To increase your chances of a positive reply, be as specific as possible.

6. Click the **Send** button to send your InMail. If the recipient doesn't respond to the InMail within seven days, the message expires.

For more information about InMail, refer to "Understanding InMail, Introductions, and LinkedIn Messages" earlier in this lesson and also refer to Lesson 1.

TIP: **Consider Alternatives to InMail**
Although InMail is an effective LinkedIn communication tool, it comes at a price. If you want to contact someone you don't know and don't want to pay to send InMail, you have several other options. You could join a group that this person belongs to and then send a message or invitation to connect as a fellow group member. You could also request an introduction through a mutual connection. Alternatively, you could choose to contact the individual outside LinkedIn by accessing the website links and external email information individuals provide on their profiles.

Requesting Introductions

Requesting an introduction is a good way to connect with people in your network whom you don't connect with directly. Although you can send an invitation to someone you don't know, you might want to consider requesting an introduction through a shared connection for important communications. An introduction can carry more weight than a cold contact.

For example, let's say that you're connected to your former manager Felice (1st degree connection) and Felice is connected to Dalton (2nd degree connection), a manager at another local company. You're very interested in working in Dalton's department, but you don't know him and haven't seen any posted job openings. Rather than sending Dalton an email and resume as a cold contact, you could send an introduction request through Felice.

Often you'll know already how you're connected to the person you want to reach, but you can also determine this by viewing the How You're Connected To [First Name] section in the right column of your target contact's profile. If you don't already know of a common connection, this section could list a name you recognize.

Here are several tips for making the most of LinkedIn introductions:

▶ **Talk to your 1st degree connection before sending an introduction request on LinkedIn**—Your connection might have information that's pertinent to your request. For example, if you're trying to reach someone about job opportunities, your connection might know whether your target is hiring or whether there's a more suitable person to contact.

▶ **Focus on introductions to 2nd degree connections for best results**—Although you can request an introduction to a 3rd degree connection, this requires two intermediaries. In many cases, the second intermediary (your 2nd degree connection passing on your request to your 3rd degree connection) might not even know you.

▶ **Make your introduction request concise and specific**—A vague request to "get to know" someone isn't nearly as effective as stating your specific purpose, such as seeking employment, recruiting for a job, offering consulting services, and so forth.

▶ **Keep in mind that LinkedIn provides only five introductions per month with a free basic account**—You can find out how many introductions you still have available on the Account & Settings page (go to the global navigation bar, click the down arrow to the left of your name, and select **Settings** from the drop-down menu). To increase your number of open introductions, you need to upgrade to a premium account. LinkedIn recommends using introductions judiciously rather than as a tool to contact hundreds of members.

To request an introduction, follow these steps:

1. Click the **Get Introduced Through a Connection** link on the profile of the person you want to reach. Remember that this link displays only for people who are your 2nd or 3rd degree connections.

2. In the Introduction Request dialog box (see Figure 6.7), select the person from whom you want to request the introduction. If you have only one connection in common with the individual you want to reach, only that connection displays in this box.

3. In the Subject field, enter the subject of your request.

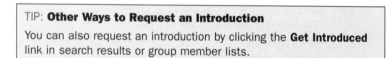

FIGURE 6.7   Requesting an introduction to someone one of your connections knows.

4. In the text box, enter your message to the person you want to be introduced to. It's also a good idea to add a brief note to the person you want to make the referral (your 1st degree connection).

5. Click the **Send Request** button to send your introduction request.

TIP: **Other Ways to Request an Introduction**

You can also request an introduction by clicking the **Get Introduced** link in search results or group member lists.

Your 1st degree connection receives your request and can choose to forward it to your target connection with comments or decline your request. If your request wasn't clear, your connection might ask you for more information.

See the following section, "Managing Introduction Requests," for more information about the next step in the process.

Managing Introduction Requests

In addition to requesting your own introductions to others, you might also receive introduction requests. For example, LinkedIn members might ask you to facilitate an introduction to one of your connections or might ask your connection to facilitate an introduction to you.

To review and respond to introduction requests, follow these steps:

1. On the global navigation bar, click the **Inbox** link to open your inbox.

2. Click the **All Messages** link and select Introductions from the drop-down menu. Your inbox displays only your introduction requests.

3. To open the request, click the subject line link. Figure 6.8 illustrates a sample introduction request.

FIGURE 6.8   Forward on an introduction request to one of your connections.

4. Click the **Forward** button to forward the request to your connection.

> NOTE: **Declining an Introduction Request**
>
> If you don't want to make the introduction, click the **Decline** button, select a reason why you feel the introduction isn't a good fit, and click the **Send** button. The person who requested the introduction will receive your feedback on why you declined the introduction.

5. Enter any additional comments on the Compose Your Message page and click the **Forward Message** button.

The target recipient receives your forwarded introduction request and can accept or decline it. Accepting the introduction enables the requestor and target to communicate with each other, but they still need to send an invitation request to become connections.

Summary

In this lesson, you learned about the many ways to communicate with other LinkedIn members and the options available based on their connection to you. Next, you learn how to search for people on LinkedIn.

LESSON 7

Searching on LinkedIn

In this lesson, you learn about LinkedIn quick searches, searching for people, advanced search techniques, and the Profile Organizer.

Performing a Quick Search

LinkedIn is a large, complex network of information. You can greatly improve your chances of achieving your networking goals by learning how to find exactly what you want among millions of member profiles and many more millions of answers, job postings, and group discussions. The easiest way to search for information on LinkedIn is to use the search box on LinkedIn's global navigation bar, shown in Figure 7.1.

FIGURE 7.1   Quickly search for information from anywhere on LinkedIn.

To perform a quick search, follow these steps:

1. Select the focus of your search from the drop-down list. Options include searching for people (the default), updates, jobs, companies, answers, your inbox, and groups.

2. Enter your search term in the text box. This might be a person's name, company name, job title, job skill, or a keyword, for example.

3. Click the **Search** button (a small white magnifying glass on a blue button). LinkedIn displays search results. The format of the search results depends on the type of search you perform.

This lesson focuses on LinkedIn's most popular search type (the people search) and advanced search techniques. To learn more about searching for jobs, companies, answers, your inbox, and groups, refer to the lessons in this book that cover those topics.

Searching for People

The fastest way to search for people is to perform a quick search from the search box on LinkedIn's global navigation bar. For example, let's say that you're searching for your former colleague Felice Mantei. Enter her name in the search box and click the **Search** button. Your search results appear, shown in Figure 7.2.

FIGURE 7.2   It's easy to find colleagues and classmates on LinkedIn.

NOTE: **LinkedIn Helps You Find Matches as You Type**

As you type, LinkedIn displays a drop-down list of potential matches in your network of connections. If you see a match in this list, click the member's name to open that member's profile.

Each LinkedIn member who matches your search results appears in a preview box that includes a photo, name, headline, location, industry, and information about shared connections and groups. Depending on the preview you're viewing, not all items might appear. For example, a member might choose not to upload a photo.

Icons appear to the right of each member's name indicating their connection to you, such as a 1st degree connection, 2nd degree connection, 3rd degree connection, or group member. For members who are out of your network, you might view the Out of Your Network designation next to their name or their name might be hidden from view. If your own name appears in search results, the YOU icon displays.

Refer to Lesson 6, "Communicating with Other LinkedIn Members," for a reminder of how LinkedIn classifies its members.

For each person, LinkedIn displays a button (such as Message, Send InMail, or Connect) as well as a drop-down list with other options (Share Profile, Find References, Get Introduced, and so forth). The options available depend on your connection to the particular person. For example, the Message button displays only for people who are your first degree connections; the Connect button or InMail button displays for everyone else. Refer to Lesson 6 for more information about the available options for contacting others on LinkedIn.

> NOTE: **LinkedIn Limits the Number of Members You Can View**
>
> With a personal account, you can view 100 results at a time. To view more results, you need to upgrade to a premium account. To learn more about premium accounts, click the **Upgrade Your Account** link on the bottom navigation menu.

Narrowing People Search Results

When you search for the name of a specific individual, the search results should display a short list (unless the individual has a very common name). But what if you can't remember someone's last name or you're searching for LinkedIn members who meet specific criteria, such as CPAs in the Indianapolis area? In this case, your search might return hundreds or even thousands of results, exceeding the 100-result viewing limits associated with a personal account.

There are two ways to handle this. One is to narrow the results that display on your search results page. The other is to perform an advanced search that targets very specific criteria.

On the search results page, you can sort the search results using the following criteria:

▶ **Relevance**—Displays search results in the order LinkedIn determines most appropriate based on keywords you enter and your network.

▶ **Relationship**—Displays search results based on their position in your network, in the following order: 1st degree connections, 2nd degree connections, fellow group members, and 3rd degree connections that are combined with out-of-network connections.

▶ **Relationship + Recommendations**—Displays search results by relationship. Those that have the most recommendations are listed first for each relationship category.

▶ **Connections**—Displays search results based on the number of common connections.

▶ **Keyword**—Displays search results that match your keywords without considering their placement in your network.

You can also customize the member information you preview in your search results. The options are

▶ **Basic**—Displays a photo, name, professional headline, location, industry, and details about shared connections.

▶ **Expanded**—Displays all the information from the basic view and current and past employment details.

The other way to narrow search results is to click the More link in the Search box to display additional options for narrowing your search, as shown in Figure 7.3.

In this box, you can narrow your search results by specifying any of the following criteria:

▶ **Keywords**—Enter a keyword that LinkedIn searches for in member profiles. The best keywords are terms that don't fit any of the other search criteria and are specific words that a member might include on a profile. For example, entering a name or location wouldn't be appropriate here, but terms such as *Java*, *PMP*, *auditing*, *CPA*, and so forth would work well.

▶ **First Name**—Enter the first name of the member you want to find.

▶ **Last Name**—Enter the last name of the member you want to find.

▶ **Title**—Enter a job title and specify any filters in the drop-down list. Options include Current or Past, Current, Past, or Past Not Current.

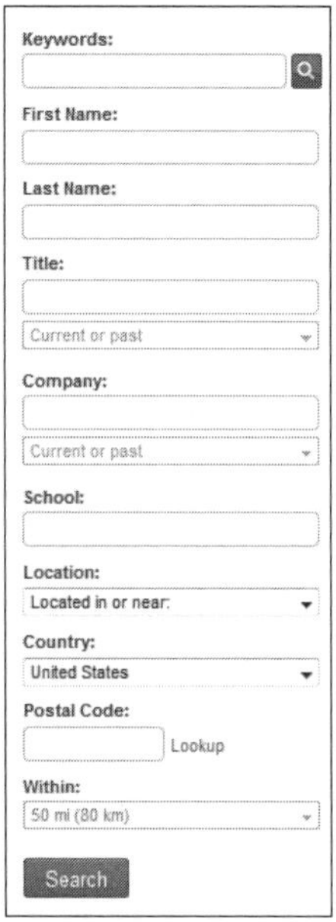

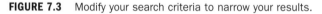

FIGURE 7.3   Modify your search criteria to narrow your results.

▶ **Company**—Enter a company name and specify any filters in the drop-down list. Options include Current or Past, Current, Past, or Past Not Current.

▶ **School**—Enter the name of a college or university.

▶ **Location**—Select a country, postal code, and distance range.

Click the **Search** button to update the search results.

For even more search options, consider the choices below the Search box. You can refine search results by company, relationship, location, industry, past company, school, or profile language. If you have a premium account, LinkedIn offers even more advanced search options such as Groups, Years of Experience, Function, Seniority Level, Interested In, Company Size, Fortune 1000, and Recently Joined. Again, click the **Search** button to update results.

Performing an Advanced People Search

If you want to search for very specific criteria, you can perform an advanced people search. An advanced search offers you the same options as the extended version of the Search box on the search results page, but you can perform it all in one step. For example, you might enter a search term in the quick search box and then decide to narrow your results. But if you already know that you want to search for specific keywords, companies, or locations, for example, an advanced search is a more streamlined option.

To perform an advanced people search, select the **People** option (if it's not already selected by default) to the left of the search box that appears on the global navigation bar and click the **Advanced** link. Figure 7.4 shows the Advanced People Search page.

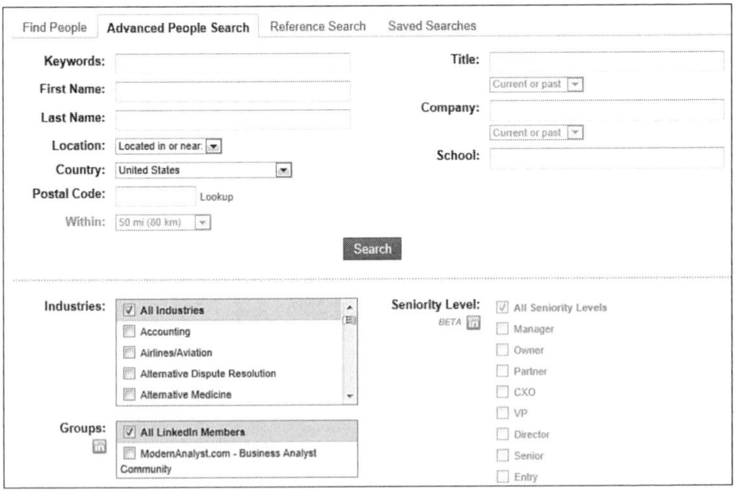

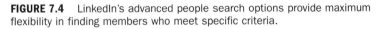

FIGURE 7.4   LinkedIn's advanced people search options provide maximum flexibility in finding members who meet specific criteria.

Enter your search criteria on this page and click the **Search** button to display your search results. Refer to "Narrowing People Search Results," earlier in this lesson, for descriptions of each field on this page.

> NOTE: **Performing a Reference Search**
>
> From the Advanced People Search page, you can click the **Reference Search** tab to search for potential references for a job candidate. See Lesson 16, "Recruiting Job Candidates," for more information about reference searches.

Saving a People Search

If you perform the same searches frequently, saving them can reduce redundant data entry. To save a search for future use, follow these steps:

1. Click the **Save Search** link on the search results page.

2. In the Save This People Search dialog box, enter a search name for this search (see Figure 7.5).

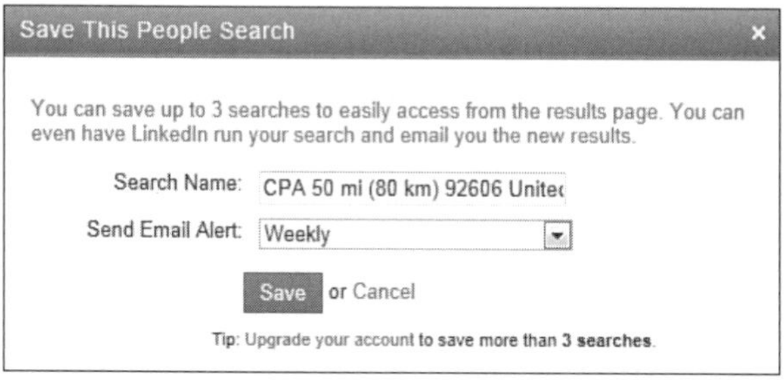

FIGURE 7.5   Saving a search saves you time.

3. In the Send Email Alert field, choose to receive email updates of your search results: Weekly, Monthly, or Never. You don't have to receive updates by email, but this can be a time-saver if you're very interested in following updates to your saved search. For example, recruiters might want to know about new LinkedIn members who match specific search criteria. Or job seekers might want to know about new LinkedIn members who work at companies they're interested in working for.

NOTE: **LinkedIn Limits the Number of Searches You Can Save**
As a free basic account holder, you can save up to three searches and receive email updates either weekly or monthly. To save more searches, click the **Upgrade Your Account** link to sign up for a premium account. If you want to receive daily email updates on your saved searches, you must select the Pro account option.

4. Click the **Save** button to save your search.

5. Click the **Close This Window** link to close the dialog box.

To edit or delete your saved searches, click the **Saved Searches** link on the search results page.

Using Advanced Search Techniques

LinkedIn offers several techniques for narrowing your search results even further. You can use these techniques when performing a quick search or when using the Advanced People Search page. For example, you can search for phrases in quotation marks, use search operators such as NOT and OR, or enter complex criteria with a parenthetical search.

LinkedIn enables you to use specific search operators to define advanced criteria directly in the quick search box. For example, *ccompany* is the operator for current company and *title* is the operator for job title. Entering **ccompany:Google title:director** would quickly list all current Google employees with the title of director.

For more information about advanced search techniques, visit the LinkedIn Learning Center at http://learn.linkedin.com/linkedin-search. Scroll down the page to the Advanced Search Tips section.

Using the Profile Organizer

LinkedIn's Profile Organizer enables you to save profiles of interest, sort them into folders, and add notes about your contact with the members whose profiles you save. This feature is particularly useful for recruiters, active job seekers, or people using LinkedIn for business development. You must have a premium LinkedIn premium account, Sales Professional, or Talent Finder account to use this tool. Depending on the plan you choose, you can maintain from 5 to 75 Profile Organizer folders.

Figure 7.6 shows a sample Profile Organizer view.

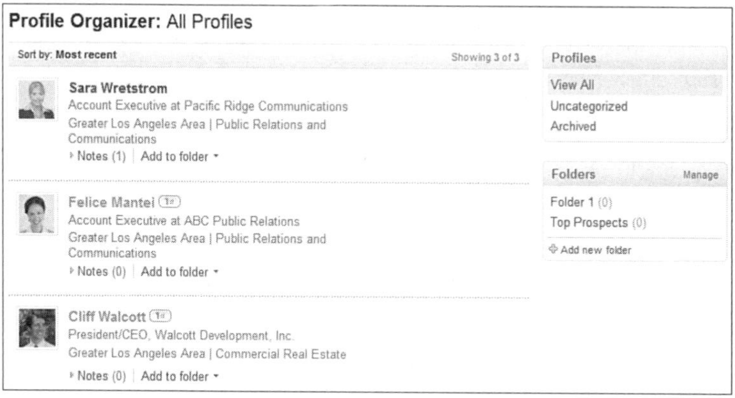

FIGURE 7.6   Save and manage LinkedIn member profiles with the Profile Organizer.

In the Profile Organizer, you can do the following:

▶ **Add and view notes about each person whose profile you saved**—Notes can contain up to 1,000 characters. This is a good place to flag profiles for follow-up, indicate where you met a particular contact, and so forth.

▶ **Add profiles to folders**—For example, you might want to create folders for potential recruitment prospects, potential clients, people you met at a conference, hiring managers at companies you want to work for, and so forth.

▶ **Contact a LinkedIn member whose profile you saved**—To view potential options, pause your mouse over the profile and view the contact options on the right side of the profile preview box. Depending on your connection to the person and what actions you've already taken, possible options include the following links: Send Message, Send InMail, Add Contact Info, Contact Information, Add a Note, Archive, and Delete.

To access Profile Organizer, select **Profile Organizer** from the Profile drop-down menu on the global navigation bar. Click the **Upgrade Now** button to upgrade to a paid account that offers profile organizer folders

---

NOTE: **Consider Free Alternatives to the Profile Organizer**

Free alternatives to the Profile Organizer include the Bookmark Profile features available with the LinkedIn Firefox browser toolbar and the LinkedIn Internet Explorer toolbar. Although bookmarking profiles in your browser doesn't offer the advanced features and flexibility of the Profile Organizer, it is a viable alternative for those on a tight budget.

Summary

In this lesson, you learned how to find information quickly and easily through LinkedIn's advanced search capabilities. Next, you learn about several tools that also enhance searching and other aspects of your LinkedIn experience.

LESSON 8

Using LinkedIn Tools

In this lesson, you learn about the tools that enable you to maximize your time on LinkedIn and integrate with other websites and software.

Understanding LinkedIn Tools

The LinkedIn Tools page offers several tools, toolbars, and widgets that enhance your LinkedIn experience, both on and off the site. Options include

- **Browser Toolbar**—Search and access LinkedIn data from Firefox or Internet Explorer.

- **JobsInsider**—Discover members of your LinkedIn network who work at companies whose job postings you're viewing. JobsInsider is included with the Browser Toolbar.

- **Outlook Social Connector**—Manage your LinkedIn network from Microsoft Outlook 2003, 2007, or 2010.

- **Email Signature**—Create a customized email signature from your profile data to use with popular email systems.

- **Google Toolbar Assistant**—Add a LinkedIn search button to the Google Toolbar.

- **Mac Search Widget**—Search LinkedIn from your Mac Dashboard.

- **Mobile**—Access your LinkedIn network via mobile devices, such as the iPhone, Android, BlackBerry, and Palm Pre. See Lesson 15, "Using LinkedIn Mobile," for more information.

▶ **LinkedIn Widget for Lotus Notes**—Integrate your LinkedIn content with Lotus Notes.

You can access LinkedIn tools by clicking the **Tools** link on the bottom navigation menu.

This lesson describes some of the most popular LinkedIn tools in more detail.

Installing and Using the LinkedIn Firefox Browser Toolbar

The LinkedIn Firefox Browser Toolbar, also called the LinkedIn Companion for Firefox, is available for a PC or Mac running Firefox versions 2.0 or 3.0. System requirements include Windows XP/Vista or Mac OS X 10.2 or later.

> TIP: **Mac Users Should Also Consider the Mac Search Widget**
> Another option for Mac users is the Mac Search Widget, which enables you to search LinkedIn from your Mac Dashboard. The widget requires OS 10.4. To download the widget, click the **Tools** link on LinkedIn's bottom navigation menu and then click the **Download It Now** button in the Mac Search Widget section.

To install the LinkedIn Firefox Browser Toolbar, follow these steps:

1. Click the **Tools** link on the bottom navigation menu.

2. In the Browser Toolbar box, pause your mouse over the **Download It Now** button and select **Firefox (Macintosh and PC)** from the drop-down menu.

3. Click the **Install Now** button in the window that appears. Depending on your operating system, you might have to allow Firefox to install this application.

4. Restart Firefox to complete your changes.

Firefox displays a welcome screen and the toolbar now appears on the menu (see Figure 8.1).

FIGURE 8.1   Use the LinkedIn Firefox Browser toolbar to locate information on LinkedIn.

If the LinkedIn button doesn't appear on your browser toolbar, try one of the following:

- ▶ Verify that you meet all the listed system requirements.

- ▶ Click the **View** menu, click **Toolbars**, and then click **LinkedIn** to display the LinkedIn toolbar on Firefox.

- ▶ Click the **View** menu, click **Toolbars**, and then click **Customize**. In the Customize Toolbars dialog box, select **Icons and Text** from the Show drop-down list, drag the LinkedIn Companion icon to the toolbar, and click the **Done** button.

Click the **LinkedIn** button on your browser toolbar to display a drop-down list of options. These include links to open your LinkedIn home page, find jobs, find people, view your contacts, add connections, and more.

To uninstall the toolbar, select **Tools**, **Add-Ons** from the Firefox menu and click the **Uninstall** button in the LinkedIn Companion for Firefox section.

Installing and Using the LinkedIn Internet Explorer Toolbar

The LinkedIn Internet Explorer Toolbar is available for the PC only. Although LinkedIn lists official support for Microsoft Windows 2000/XP, with Microsoft Internet Explorer 6.0 and 7.0, you should be able to install this app on Windows Vista and Windows 7 as well.

To install the LinkedIn Internet Explorer Toolbar, follow these steps:

1. Click the **Tools** link on the bottom navigation menu.

2. In the Browser Toolbar box, pause your mouse over the **Download It Now** button and select **Internet Explorer (PC Only)** from the drop-down menu.

3. Click the **Run** button. The LinkedIn Internet Explorer Toolbar Setup dialog box opens.

4. Click the **Next** button to continue.

5. Select the check box to accept the license agreement and click the **Next** button.

6. Accept the default installation folder and click the **Install** button. Alternatively, click the **Browse** button to select another folder.

7. A warning dialog box prompts you to close all open Internet Explorer windows. Do so, and click the **Yes** button to continue.

8. Select the **Launch Internet Explorer with LinkedIn Toolbar** check box and click the **Finish** button.

Internet Explorer opens with the toolbar installed, shown in Figure 8.2.

NOTE: **Where Is the LinkedIn Toolbar?**

If the LinkedIn Toolbar doesn't appear, click the **Tools** icon on the Internet Explorer toolbar and select **Manage Add-Ons** from the menu. In the Manage Add-Ons dialog box, you can verify that the LinkedIn Toolbar is enabled. Also verify that you meet the system requirements to install the toolbar.

FIGURE 8.2   Search, access, and bookmark pages from LinkedIn while using Internet Explorer.

Click the down arrow to the right of the **LinkedIn** button on your browser toolbar to display a drop-down list of options. These include links to open your LinkedIn home page, find jobs, find people, view your contacts, add connections, and more.

To remove the LinkedIn Internet Explorer Toolbar, go to the Control Panel and delete it. The exact path to access the Control Panel varies by operating system.

Using JobsInsider

LinkedIn JobsInsider is a LinkedIn Browser Toolbar feature that assists in your job search. When you're viewing a job posting, JobsInsider lets you know about LinkedIn members in your network who work at that company and are potential inside connections for you. JobsInsider works with job postings on sites such as Monster, CareerBuilder, HotJobs, Craigslist, Simply Hired, Dice, and Vault.

NOTE: **You Must Install the LinkedIn Browser Toolbar to Use JobsInsider**

If you haven't installed the LinkedIn Browser Toolbar yet, click the JobsInsider link on the bottom navigation menu for installation instructions. See the "Installing and Using the LinkedIn Firefox Browser Toolbar" and the "Installing and Using the LinkedIn Internet Explorer Toolbar" sections earlier in this lesson for more information.

For example, if you're searching Monster.com for potential jobs, JobsInsider opens automatically, detecting that you're searching a job site. Figure 8.3 shows a sample view of JobsInsider.

FIGURE 8.3   JobsInsider points out your inside connections at a hiring company.

When you open a job posting, JobsInsider lists the names of your 1st degree connections and includes links to their LinkedIn profiles. It also tells you the total people in your network who work at this company. Click the number to view a list of these people.

NOTE: **You Can Activate and Deactivate JobsInsider**

To specify JobsInsider settings, click the **LinkedIn** button on your browser toolbar and select **Preferences** from the menu. In the Preferences dialog box, you can specify whether you want to open JobsInsider when browsing a known job site, open at browser startup, or not open at all.

Using the Sharing Bookmarklet

LinkedIn offers a Sharing Bookmarklet that enables you to share content on LinkedIn from any of the following browsers: Internet Explorer, Firefox, Chrome, and Safari. Using the bookmarklet, you can easily share news stories, blog posts, and other interesting web content with LinkedIn members, including your connections and fellow members of groups.

Installing the Bookmarklet

To install the bookmarklet, follow these steps:

1. Click the **Tools** link on the bottom navigation menu.

2. Select the **Sharing Bookmarklet** tab.

3. Follow the on-screen instructions for installing the bookmarklet. The installation steps vary based on your browser. For example, Internet Explorer requires that you add the bookmarklet to your favorites menu, whereas Firefox asks that you simply drag the icon to your browser toolbar.

Sharing with the Bookmarklet

To share web pages, follow these steps:

1. In your browser, navigate to the page you want to share.

2. Click the **Share on LinkedIn** button on the toolbar. On some browsers, this is called the Share in LinkedIn button.

3. In the pop-up box that opens (see Figure 8.4), specify how you want to share this content: post as an update, post to a group, or send to individual LinkedIn members.

4. Click the **Share** button to share this web page.

If you post as an update, the content you share displays at the top of your profile and on your connections' home pages, just like a regular update.

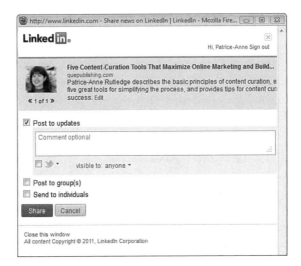

FIGURE 8.4   Share selected web pages with LinkedIn connections or group members.

CAUTION: **Share Selectively**

Although this feature provides a convenient way to share content on LinkedIn, it's a powerful tool that you shouldn't overuse. To generate a positive response from other LinkedIn members, focus on sharing only the most useful, relevant content that affects the majority of group members. For example, share a top news story or an insightful report that affects your industry. Don't share promotional material, sales pages, or your daily blog posts (unless one contains highly useful or relevant content).

Creating an Email Signature

LinkedIn enables you to create an email signature that includes links to your profile and other popular LinkedIn features. You can use your LinkedIn email signature with popular email systems such as Microsoft Outlook, Outlook Express, Mozilla Thunderbird, and Yahoo! Mail.

To create an email signature, follow these steps:

1. Click the **Tools** link on the bottom navigation menu.

2. In the Email Signature section of the LinkedIn Tools page, click the **Try It Now** button. The Create Email Signature page opens, shown in Figure 8.5.

FIGURE 8.5   Create an email signature you can use with many popular email systems.

3. Select a layout for your email signature from the drop-down list. A preview of your signature with the selected layout appears on the page. To view all the options at once, click the **View Gallery** link.

4. Enter the contact information you want to appear on your signature in the Business Information, Contact Information, and Work Address sections.

5. If you want to include a company logo or your photo, enter the image's URL in the Image Selection field. Your image must be in the GIF, JPG, or PNG format; no larger than 50KB; and no larger than 100×60 in size. Click the **Show** link to display your image. Be aware that the way you add an image could vary depending on the browser you're using.

NOTE: **You Can Use Your LinkedIn Profile Photo on Your Signature**

To use your LinkedIn photo, right-click the photo on your profile and choose **Copy Image Location** or **Copy Shortcut** from the menu. (The menu option varies by browser.) Paste (Ctrl+V) this link in the Image Selection field.

6. Select any of or all the following check boxes to place links on your email signature: **Professional Profile link**, **See Who We Know in Common link**, or **We're Hiring link**.

7. Click the **Click Here for Instructions** link to save your signature.

8. In the pop-up box that opens, copy your signature code by clicking in the text box and pressing Ctrl+C on your keyboard.

9. Select your email client from the drop-down list. Instructions for using the email signature in your email system appear.

10. Click the **Close This Window** link (at the bottom of the window) to close the window and install your new email signature.

Other LinkedIn Tools

Here's a quick roundup of even more tools and features that can enhance the time you spend on LinkedIn.

LinkedIn Today

If you want to stay on top of what's happening in your industry and are short on time, check out LinkedIn Today (see Figure 8.6) by selecting **LinkedIn Today** from the News drop-down menu on the global navigation bar.

News items from LinkedIn Today also display on your home page. LinkedIn Today shows you what people in your network and industry are currently sharing on LinkedIn and Twitter. No two members see exactly the same content on LinkedIn Today, which is why it's more relevant than scanning the headlines on a traditional online news publication.

LinkedIn Skills

LinkedIn Skills offers a great way to view the most popular skills on LinkedIn profiles, find industry leaders who possess these skills, add skills to your own profile, and even find jobs that require specific skills.

FIGURE 8.6   View personalized news, based on your LinkedIn network and profile.

To get started, select **Skills** from the More drop-down menu on the global navigation bar. Figure 8.7 shows the Skills page.

From here, you can browse the skills that display on the lower portion of the page or enter a skill in the search box and click the **Search** button.

LinkedIn Signal

If you feel overloaded with too much information on LinkedIn, Signal can help you filter to the content you most want to see. To access Signal, select **Signal** from the News drop-down menu on the global navigation bar.

On the Signal page, you can filter LinkedIn updates by network, company, location, industry, time, group, topic, and more.

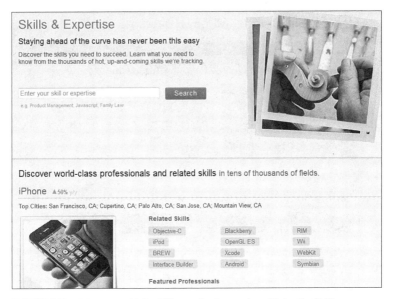

FIGURE 8.7   Discover which skills are in demand on LinkedIn Skills.

LinkedIn Share Button

If you publish content on a website or blog, encourage your readers to share this content on LinkedIn by adding the LinkedIn Share button to your site. This button is similar to the Facebook and Twitter buttons that are popular on so many blogs and can be a big help in generating more visibility and traffic.

To get your LinkedIn Share button, visit http://www.linkedin.com/publishers. The LinkedIn Share button is available in three different formats: vertical count (the number of shares displays above the button), horizontal count (the number of shares displays to the right of the button), and no count (button only with no numbers). Copy and paste the code on this page into your own site's HTML to install.

LinkedIn InMaps

Ever want to view a visual map of your entire LinkedIn network? LinkedIn InMaps enables you to do just that. To access your InMap, visit http://inmaps.linkedinlabs.com while signed in to LinkedIn. For your InMap to provide meaningful data, you must have at least 50 connections and at least 75% of your profile complete. If you meet these requirements, your InMap displays a color-coded representation of your LinkedIn network that you can zoom to view in more detail, label, and share with your network.

LinkedIn Swarm

LinkedIn Swarm (http://swarm.linkedinlabs.com) is another visual LinkedIn tool. With Swarm, you can view a moving tag cloud of LinkedIn activity over the past hour. Swarm analyzes company and title searches, jobs posted, blog entries, and shared articles. In other words, it provides real-time insight into what's hot and trending on LinkedIn.

Summary

In this lesson, you learned how to install and use tools that help you maximize your LinkedIn experience and integrate with other popular websites and software programs. Next, learn how to find a job using LinkedIn.

LESSON 9

Finding a Job

In this lesson, you learn how to use LinkedIn as an effective job search tool, find and apply to job postings, and use LinkedIn's many other features for job seekers.

Attracting Recruiters and Hiring Managers

LinkedIn is an excellent tool for job seekers, but you need to create a stellar profile and develop a solid network if you want to maximize your results. Here are seven tips for making the most of LinkedIn as a job search tool.

▶ **Complete your profile**—LinkedIn reports that members with a complete profile generate 40 times more opportunities than those whose profiles aren't complete.

▶ **Develop a solid network of connections**—Your ability to use job search features such as JobsInsider and Inside Connections depends on having a reasonable number of connections. You should aim for at least 50 connections to maximize the benefits of these features, although they do work with fewer connections.

▶ **Get recommendations**—A complete profile includes at least three recommendations. Aim for recommendations from managers, executives, or actual clients. Peer recommendations, particularly those that you "trade" with colleagues by recommending each other, carry far less weight.

▶ **Include keywords that are relevant to your profession and industry**—These include specific skills, certifications, and degrees. Recruiters search for these words, and your profile should include them if you want to be found.

▶ **Add relevant skills to your profile**—Listing your key skills on your profile makes it easier for recruiters to find you and quickly identify your skillset.

▶ **Focus on results, not a list of duties**—Remember that your profile is a concise summary of your qualifications, not a resume (although you can attach one if you like). Emphasize your results and accomplishments; don't just list tasks you performed.

▶ **Post a resume or portfolio**—Using LinkedIn applications such as Box.net Files, you can attach PDFs to your profile.

▶ **Indicate on your profile that you're seeking employment**—If you're unemployed, include this information in your status, professional headline, or summary. Don't sound desperate, but do let your network know that you're looking for opportunities.

See Lesson 2, "Creating Your Profile," and Lesson 10, "Requesting and Providing Recommendations," for more information.

TIP: **Clean Up Your Digital Dirt Before Your Job Search**

Keep in mind that many recruiters now search the Web for background information on potential candidates. It isn't enough to have a professional presence on LinkedIn. Review any other social networking profiles you have to ensure they also reinforce your professional image. If not, remove your "digital dirt" before you begin your job search. Also, verify that your contacts don't post photos or other content about you that would compromise your professional reputation.

Searching Job Postings

LinkedIn offers a large database of job postings that are posted directly on LinkedIn and on its partner site, Simply Hired.

TIP: **LinkedIn Offers Other Ways to Find Job Postings**

Although the Jobs page is LinkedIn's primary job search tool, you should also search the Jobs Discussion Board for any group you belong to and the Careers tab on the company page of your target employers. To do a quick search for jobs, use the search box on the top navigation menu.

To search job postings on LinkedIn, follow these steps:

1. On the global navigation bar, click the **Jobs** link. The Jobs page opens, shown in Figure 9.1.

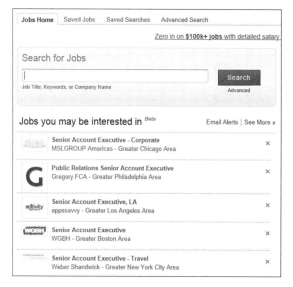

FIGURE 9.1   On the Jobs page, you can review suggested jobs based on your profile or search for jobs by keyword.

NOTE: **View Jobs LinkedIn Recommends for You**

Below the search box on the Jobs page, LinkedIn lists jobs you might be interested in based on the information you entered on your profile. For example, if you work in project management, you could view a list of jobs in this field.

2. In the Search for Jobs box, enter keywords related to your job search. For example, you could enter a job title, a job skill, or the name of a target company.

3. Click the **Search** button. The Job Search Results page opens, shown in Figure 9.2.

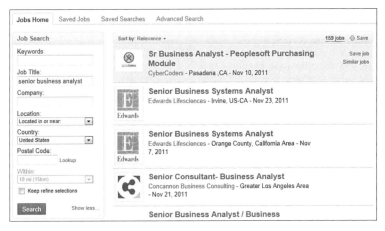

FIGURE 9.2   Viewing a list of jobs that match your criteria.

On this page, you can do the following:

▶ Sort jobs by relevance, your relationship to the job poster, or the date posted (most recent or earliest).

▶ Identify the company by its logo (not available for all postings).

▶ Open the job posting by clicking the job title link.

▶ Save this job search and have results sent to you via email on a regular basis, such as daily, weekly, or monthly.

▶ Save a specific job posting by pausing the mouse over it and clicking the **Save Job** link. You can review the jobs you save at a later time by clicking the Saved Jobs tab on the Jobs page.

▶ View jobs similar to a specific job posting by pausing the mouse over it and clicking the **Similar Jobs** link. LinkedIn displays jobs that are the most similar to the one you selected.

▶ Refine your search criteria using the fields on the left side of the page. The fields in the Job Search box are nearly identical to the fields on the Advanced Search page. See "Performing an Advanced Job Search" later in this lesson for more information.

Viewing Job Postings

The content listed on a job posting varies according to what the hiring company chooses to display. The content that you see will also vary according to what type of connection you have to the poster and the connections you have to the people working at that company. A job posting (see Figure 9.3) might include some or all of the following features:

▶ A header listing the job title, location, and company URL.

▶ A detailed job description.

▶ The Apply Now button. Click this button to apply for the job from LinkedIn. See the "Applying for a Job" section later in this lesson for more information. Alternatively, the Apply on Company Website button might display if a company prefers to use its own application process.

▶ The Save Job link. Click to save this job for future viewing on the My Jobs page.

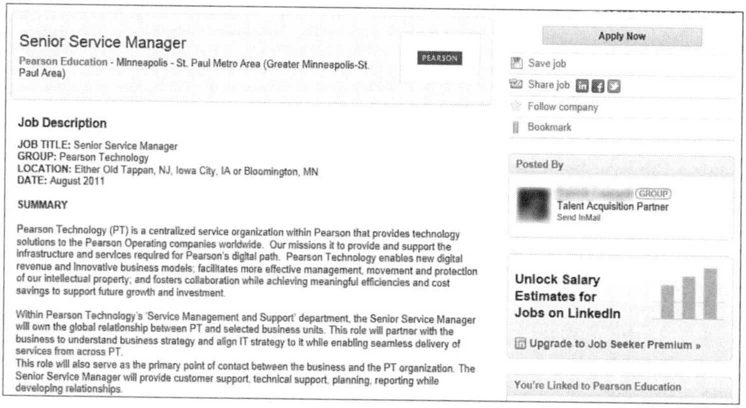

FIGURE 9.3 Viewing a list of jobs that match specified criteria.

▶ The Share Job link. Click to open the Share This Job dialog box, which enables you to send a message to a connection who might be interested in this job, share with fellow group members, or share on Facebook, Twitter, or with your LinkedIn network (displays with other network updates).

▶ The Follow Company link, which enables you to follow this company's activity on LinkedIn.

▶ The Bookmark link, which enables you to bookmark this job on Internet Explorer. You won't see this option if you aren't using Internet Explorer as your browser.

▶ The Posted By box with a link to the job poster's LinkedIn profile. A connection icon appears if this person is in your network. For example, if a job poster is connected to one of your connections, the 2nd degree connection icon appears. Depending on your connection to the job poster, a link to request an introduction or send InMail could appear. Refer to Lesson 6, "Communicating with Other LinkedIn Members," for more information about LinkedIn introductions and InMail.

▶ The You're Linked to [Company Name] box. Click one of the links in this box to display the LinkedIn members in your network who work at this company. These people could provide you inside information about potential job opportunities.

▶ The Similar Jobs box, which lists jobs that are similar to the one you're viewing.

Performing an Advanced Job Search

If you want to search for jobs based on specific criteria, try an advanced job search:

1. On the global navigation bar, click the **Jobs** link.

2. Click the **Advanced Search** tab on the Jobs page. You can also open this page by clicking the **Advanced** link when searching for jobs from the search box on the global navigation bar. Figure 9.4 shows the Advanced Search page.

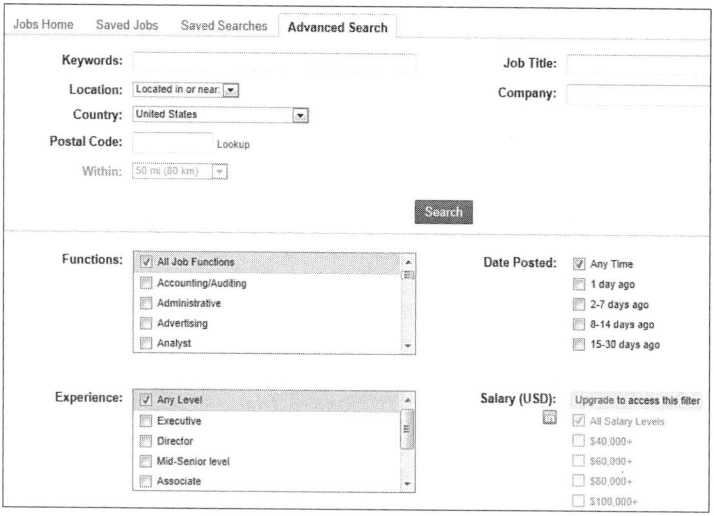

FIGURE 9.4   Performing an advanced job search.

3. In the Keywords text box, enter keywords (such as a job title, a skill, or a certification). Refer to Lesson 7, "Searching on LinkedIn," for more information on using advanced search criteria.

4. Specify the criteria for your search. For example, you can narrow your search results by location, job title, company, function, industry, experience level, date posted, or salary.

5. Click the **Search** button to display job search results.

Refer to the earlier section, "Searching Job Postings," for more information about the job search results page.

TIP: **Specify Only the Most Important Criteria**

You don't need to specify criteria in all the fields available on the Advanced Search page. Start with a few choices and then narrow or expand your search based on your search results.

Applying for a Job

LinkedIn offers two ways to apply for jobs, based on the way the company posting a job handles its recruitment. If the Apply on Company Website button displays on a job posting, clicking this button takes you to the company's external website where you can apply for the job. If the Apply Now button displays on the job posting, clicking this button directs you to a job application form on LinkedIn. In this section, you learn how to complete LinkedIn's own job application form.

To apply for a job from a LinkedIn posting, follow these steps:

1. In the job description for the job you would like to apply for, click the **Apply Now** button to open the Apply Now dialog box, as shown in Figure 9.5.

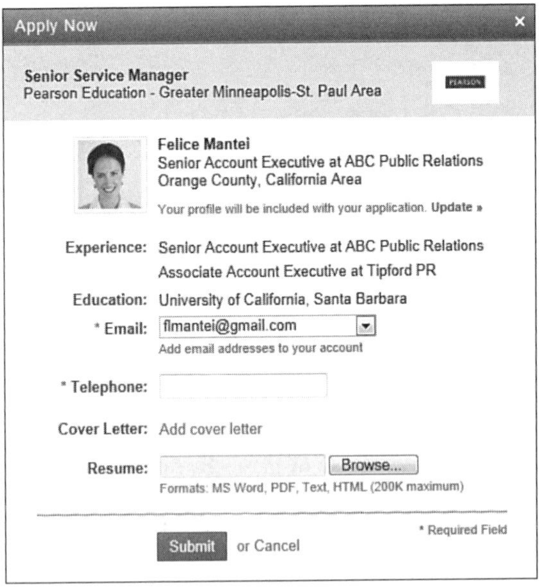

FIGURE 9.5 Applying for jobs directly from LinkedIn.

2. LinkedIn includes your profile with your application. If you need to update this data before applying, click the **Update** link to open the Edit Profile page. When you finish making changes, you can return to the Apply Now dialog box.

3. Enter a telephone number where the recruiter can reach you. If you're currently working, entering your cell phone number is often the best option.

4. Click the **Add Cover Letter** link to display a text box where you can add your cover letter. A good cover letter summarizes strengths and accomplishments that are relevant to this job and is personalized for this target job.

5. Click the **Browse** button next to the Resume field to upload your resume as a text file, Word document, PDF, or HTML file of no more than 200KB. LinkedIn attaches your uploaded resume in its original format.

6. Click the **Submit** button to submit your application for the job.

Finding Recruiters and Hiring Managers

The good news for job seekers: Thousands of recruiters and hiring managers maintain profiles on LinkedIn. To find them, select People in the quick search box on the global navigation bar. Then click the **Advanced** link to the right of the box to open the Advanced People Search page.

There are several ways to find recruiters and hiring managers on the Advanced People Search page. Some examples include the following:

▶ In the Industries field, select Staffing and Recruiting and enter keywords related to the type of job you're looking for. If applicable, enter location criteria.

▶ Enter Recruiter in the Title field and the name of a company you want to work for.

▶ Enter Recruiter in the Title field plus relevant location information.

▶ Enter the name of a company you want to work for and select Hiring Managers from the Interested In drop-down list (if you have a premium account).

Searching for appropriate contacts is a combination of art and science, so you might need to revise your search criteria several times before you find the appropriate people.

CAUTION: **Don't Spam Recruiters and Hiring Managers**

Remember that LinkedIn is a networking and research tool, not a means of spamming prospective recruiters and employers. When you do find good targets for your job search, review their profiles carefully to determine the best way to contact them. Some recruiters provide links to external sites for job candidates. If your target is a hiring manager, determine whether you can reach this person through a network introduction. Alternatively, consider sending a brief message to hiring managers who indicate they are open to job inquiries.

Upgrading to a Job Seeker Premium Account

LinkedIn offers many free features and opportunities for job seekers. If you need access to LinkedIn premium features to aid in your job search, however, consider upgrading to a Job Seeker premium account. For example, these accounts can provide access to InMail and the OpenLink Network and increase your available introductions.

All Job Seeker premium accounts enable you to display a Job Seeker badge on your profile, receive placement as a featured applicant when you apply for a job, use premium search features, view who is interested in your profile, participate in the OpenLink Network (described in Lesson 1, "Introducing LinkedIn"), and receive priority customer service from LinkedIn.

Table 9.1 shows the specific features for each level of Job Seeker account.

To upgrade to a Job Seeker premium account or learn more about upgrade options, select **Job Seeker Premium** from the Jobs drop-down menu on the global navigation bar.

TABLE 9.1   Job Seeker Account Comparison

Feature	Basic	Job Seeker	Job Seeker Plus
Monthly Price	$19.95	$29.95	$49.95
InMails	None	5	10
Pending Introductions	10	15	25

Summary

In this lesson, you learned about LinkedIn's many job search tools. In addition, you learned the most effective way to conduct a job search on LinkedIn. Next, learn how to request and provide recommendations on LinkedIn.

LESSON 10

Requesting and Providing Recommendations

In this lesson, you learn how to request, provide, manage, and revise professional recommendations on LinkedIn.

Understanding LinkedIn Recommendations

LinkedIn enables you to request recommendations from and provide recommendations to the people in your professional network. Recommendations are a powerful networking tool, so consider carefully whom you want to ask for a recommendation and whom you want to recommend as part of your overall LinkedIn strategy.

LinkedIn offers four types of recommendations:

- ▶ **Colleague**—You worked with this person at the same company as a manager, peer, or employee.

- ▶ **Business Partner**—You worked with this person in another capacity, not as a colleague or client. For example, you worked at partner companies, performed volunteer or association work together, and so forth.

- ▶ **Student**—You were a teacher, advisor, or fellow student at the same school.

- ▶ **Service Provider**—You hired this person to perform services.

The recommendation process involves several steps between two people to ensure that both approve the recommendation before it is final. For example, if Oliver wants to request a recommendation from his former manager, Sophie—a common type of request—the process requires four steps:

> ▶ **Step 1**—Oliver sends a recommendation request to Sophie.

> ▶ **Step 2**—Sophie receives the request and submits a recommendation for Oliver.

> ▶ **Step 3**—Oliver receives a notification about Sophie's recommendation and accepts the recommendation.

> ▶ **Step 4**—LinkedIn displays the recommendation on Oliver's profile.

Obviously, this process assumes that both Oliver and Sophie approve each step. LinkedIn also offers options for you to request clarifications and changes. If you write an unsolicited recommendation for a connection without receiving a recommendation request, your process starts at step 2 with submitting the recommendation.

Requesting Recommendations

Receiving recommendations from managers, colleagues, and clients can help you achieve your networking goals on LinkedIn. LinkedIn suggests that a complete profile should include at least three recommendations for maximum effectiveness.

Before you send your requests, however, think about what you want to achieve. Be clear about your goals so that your connections write recommendations that help you achieve them. For example, if you want to move into a management position, you should request a recommendation that discusses your leadership abilities. If you want to change careers, emphasize crossover skills.

> TIP: **Let Your Connections Know You Want a Recommendation**
> Although LinkedIn notifies your connections that you've requested a recommendation, it's a good idea that this message doesn't come

as a surprise. Talk to the people you want to recommend you so that they're aware of your request and know what to emphasize in their recommendation.

To request a recommendation from one of your connections, follow these steps:

1. On the global navigation bar, select **Recommendations** from the Profile drop-down menu. The Received Recommendations page opens, shown in Figure 10.1.

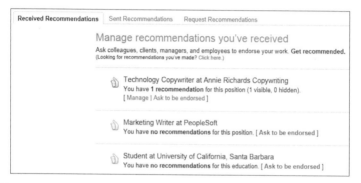

Received Recommendations   Sent Recommendations   Request Recommendations

Manage recommendations you've received

Ask colleagues, clients, managers, and employees to endorse your work. **Get recommended.**
(Looking for recommendations you've made? Click here.)

Technology Copywriter at Annie Richards Copywriting
You have **1 recommendation** for this position (1 visible, 0 hidden).
[Manage | Ask to be endorsed]

Marketing Writer at PeopleSoft
You have **no recommendations** for this position. [Ask to be endorsed]

Student at University of California, Santa Barbara
You have **no recommendations** for this education. [Ask to be endorsed]

FIGURE 10.1   Ask your connections for professional recommendations to enhance your profile.

2. Click the **Ask to Be Endorsed** link next to the related position or school. The Request Recommendations page opens, shown in Figure 10.2.

TIP: **Keep Your Profile Up to Date**

The Received Recommendations page displays only positions and schools you've already entered on your profile. If you haven't done this, click the **Add a Job** or **Add a School** link to complete this step first.

NOTE: **Request a Recommendation from Your Profile**

You can also request a recommendation on the **Edit Profile** page. To do so, click the **Ask for Recommendations** or **Request**

Recommendations link below the related position or school in the Experience or Education section. If you already have at least one recommendation, this link is called the Manage link.

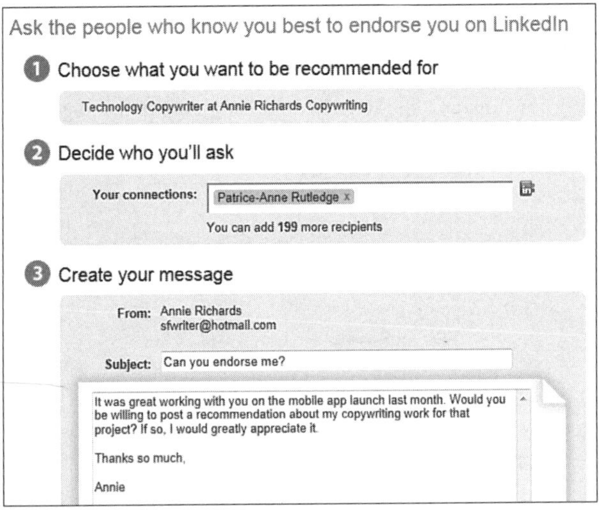

Ask the people who know you best to endorse you on LinkedIn

1 Choose what you want to be recommended for

Technology Copywriter at Annie Richards Copywriting

2 Decide who you'll ask

Your connections: Patrice-Anne Rutledge x

You can add **199 more recipients**

3 Create your message

From: Annie Richards
       sfwriter@hotmail.com

Subject: Can you endorse me?

It was great working with you on the mobile app launch last month. Would you be willing to post a recommendation about my copywriting work for that project? If so, I would greatly appreciate it.

Thanks so much,

Annie

FIGURE 10.2   Requesting a recommendation is a simple process.

3. In step 1, the position or school you selected appears by default. To change this, return to the previous page.

4. In step 2, start typing the name of the connection you want to ask for a recommendation. Select the correct name from the drop-down list of options that appear.

CAUTION: **Don't Mass Produce Recommendation Requests**
Although you can request a recommendation from up to 200 connections at a time, it's a much better practice to personalize each recommendation request you send. If you really want to send your request to more than one person, however, click the **View All Connections** button to select your recipients.

5. In step 3, create your message asking for a recommendation. LinkedIn provides sample text for you, but you should customize this for each request. Be specific and let your connection know what you want to achieve with this recommendation. You don't need to add a salutation; LinkedIn does this automatically.

6. Click the **Send** button. LinkedIn sends your recommendation request to its target recipient. If you selected more than one person in step 2, each person receives an individual message.

See "Managing Recommendation Requests" to learn what happens when a connection receives your recommendation request.

Managing Recommendation Requests

After you send a recommendation request, the Received Recommendations tab indicates that you have a pending request. This text remains until your connection submits a recommendation for you.

To review your request, click the **Manage** link below the related position or school. The Manage Received Recommendations page opens, shown in Figure 10.3.

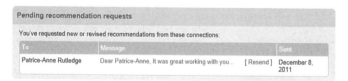

FIGURE 10.3   Review your pending recommendation requests.

On this page, you can view a list of the recommendations you've requested and the date you requested them. If your request has been pending for more than a week, click the **Resend** link to send your request again with a message to the recipient. It's also a good idea to contact this person directly.

Responding to Recommendation Requests

LinkedIn sends a message to your inbox when you receive recommendation requests. The default subject line for these messages is "Can You Endorse Me?" unless the person requesting the recommendation modifies this text.

To respond to a recommendation request, follow these steps:

1. On the global navigation bar, click the **Inbox** link. Refer to Lesson 6, "Communicating with Other LinkedIn Members," for more information about working with your inbox.

2. Select the message that contains the recommendation request. Figure 10.4 illustrates a sample recommendation request.

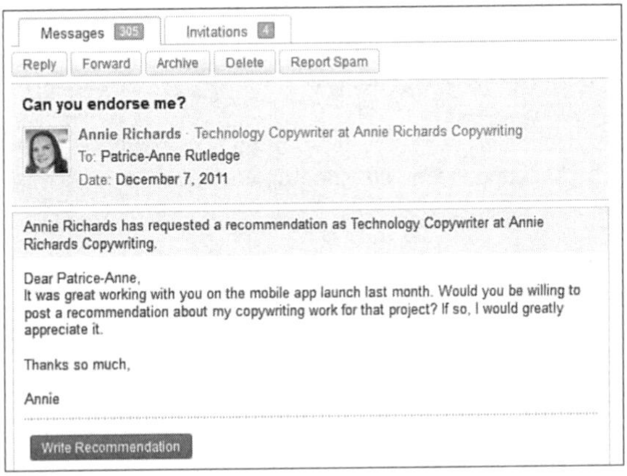

FIGURE 10.4   LinkedIn notifies you every time you receive a recommendation request.

3. Click the **Write Recommendation** button to write your recommendation. The Select Type page opens, shown in Figure 10.5.

> **Annie Richards** is requesting a recommendation for work done as **Technology Copywriter at Annie Richards Copywriting**
>
> ❝ Recommend Annie as a:
>
>   ◎ **Colleague:** You've worked with Annie at the same company
>   ◎ **Service Provider:** You've hired Annie to provide a service for you or your company
>   ◎ **Business Partner:** You've worked with Annie, but not as a client or colleague
>
> [Continue]

FIGURE 10.5   Your options vary depending on the recommendation type you choose.

NOTE: LinkedIn Handles Student Requests Differently

If this is for a student request, LinkedIn doesn't ask you to select a recommendation type and opens the Create Your Recommendation page directly.

---

4. If this recommendation is for a position, select from the following options: Colleague, Service Provider, or Business Partner. Refer to "Understanding LinkedIn Recommendations," earlier in this lesson, for more information about these recommendation types.

5. Click the **Continue** button to open the Create Your Recommendation page, shown in Figure 10.6.

6. The fields in the top portion of the Create Your Recommendation page vary based on your selection in step 4. In general, this section asks you to specify how you know this person.

7. Enter your recommendation in the Written Recommendation box. LinkedIn offers sample text, but you need to replace this with your own recommendation. Write a concise, specific recommendation that relates to the position and the goals of the person you're recommending.

8. Click the **View/Edit** link to display the Personalize This Message text box, where you can personalize the message you send to the person requesting your recommendation. This text doesn't appear on the recommendation itself.

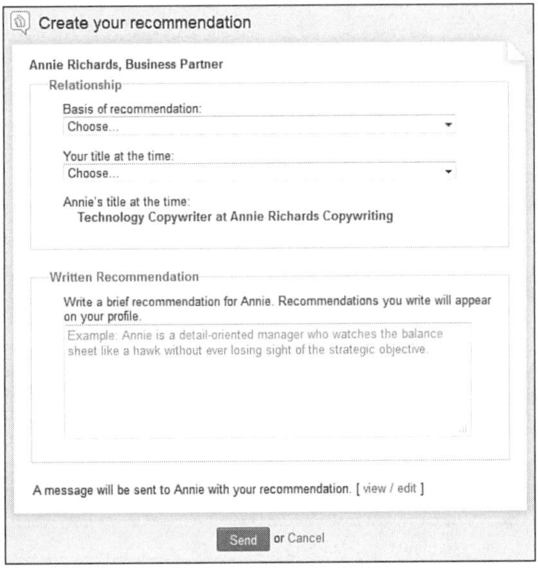

FIGURE 10.6   Create a recommendation that describes this person's accomplishments clearly and concisely.

9. Click the **Send** button to send the recommendation and accompanying message to the requestor.

TIP: **Consider Carefully Who You Recommend**

Consider carefully before recommending someone on LinkedIn. Remember that your reputation is based not only on who recommends you, but also on who you recommend. Is this someone you would recommend in the real world? If not, reply privately to the person explaining that you don't feel comfortable giving the recommendation. For example, you might not know the person well enough for a recommendation, or your experience working together might not have been a positive one.

Accepting Recommendations

When someone recommends you, LinkedIn sends a notification message to your inbox. If you indicate that you want to receive email notifications on the Account & Settings page, LinkedIn also notifies you by email.

Open the message to view the complete recommendation. Figure 10.7 illustrates a sample message.

FIGURE 10.7   Review your recommendation for accuracy before accepting it.

On this page, you can

▶ Select **Show This Recommendation on My Profile** if you want to display the recommendation.

▶ Select **Hide This Recommendation on My Profile** if you want to hide the recommendation. In general, displaying your recommendations is a good promotional tool. You should hide unsolicited recommendations you don't want others to view.

▶ Click the **Accept Recommendation** button to accept the recommendation.

▶ Click the **Request Replacement** link to ask for a revised recommendation. This option is useful if the recommendation isn't accurate, contains misspellings, or doesn't focus on your current goals or accomplishments. To ensure you receive a more appropriate recommendation, be sure to specify *why* you need a replacement.

If you accept your recommendation and choose to show it on your profile, you can view it below its related position or school.

Making Recommendations

At times, you might want to recommend your connections even if they don't send you a recommendation request. To make a recommendation, follow these steps:

1. On the global navigation bar, select **Recommendations** from the Profile drop-down menu.

2. Scroll down the Received Recommendations page to the Make a Recommendation box, shown in Figure 10.8.

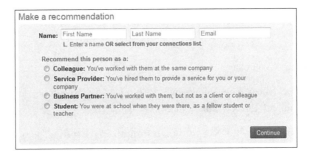

FIGURE 10.8   You can make several kinds of recommendations on LinkedIn.

TIP: **Make Recommendations from a Connection's Profile Page**
Another way to initiate a recommendation is to visit a connection's profile page and click the **Recommend** link below the related position or school, which opens the Create Your Recommendation page.

3. Click the **Select from Your Connections List** link to select your target recipient. Alternatively, enter a person's name and email address.

4. Select the type of recommendation you want to write. Options include Colleague, Service Provider, Business Partner, and Student.

5. Click the **Continue** button to open the Create Your Recommendation page.

See "Responding to Recommendation Requests" earlier in this lesson for more information on completing the Create Your Recommendation page. The process is the same whether you respond to a recommendation request or initiate it yourself.

Managing Recommendations

Several times a year, you should review your recommendations to verify that they're still relevant to your current goals. You might want to hide a recommendation that's no longer relevant or request updated recommendations from those who have recommended you in the past.

To manage your recommendations, select **Recommendations** from the Profile drop-down menu on the global navigation bar.

Managing Received Recommendations

On the Received Recommendations page, click the **Manage** link below the recommendation you want to change. To hide a recommendation from your profile, remove the check mark next to the Show check box. Click the **Save Changes** button to save this change (see Figure 10.9).

FIGURE 10.9   Review your recommendations regularly to verify that they still meet your needs.

To ask a connection for a revised recommendation, click the **Request a New or Revised Recommendation From [Person's Name]** link. LinkedIn sends a message to this connection asking for a revision. Be sure to communicate clearly what you're looking for in your revised recommendation. For example, you might want to revise a recommendation if your job duties for the same position have changed or you want to emphasize a different aspect of your job for future career growth.

> TIP: **Request a New Recommendation If You Have a New Job Title**
>
> If you receive a promotion or have a new job title, add a new position and request a recommendation for that job rather than revising an existing recommendation.

Managing Sent Recommendations

To manage the recommendations you give others, select **Recommendations** from the Profile drop-down menu on the global navigation bar. Click the **Sent Recommendations** link to open the Sent Recommendations page, shown in Figure 10.10.

On this page, you can

▶ **Change the display options for a recommendation**—By default, the recommendations you give your connections appear on your profile for all LinkedIn members to see. Click the

Display on My Profile To drop-down list and choose either Connections Only or No One to change this.

▶ **Revise a recommendation**—Click the **Edit** link next to the recommendation you want to revise and make your changes on the Edit Your Recommendation page. Click the **Send** button to make your changes and notify your connection.

▶ **Withdraw a recommendation**—Click the **Edit** link next to the recommendation you want to withdraw. On the Edit Your Recommendation page, click the **Withdraw This Recommendation** link. A pop-up box asks you to confirm that you want to withdraw the recommendation permanently.

FIGURE 10.10   Revise or withdraw a recommendation on the Sent Recommendations page.

Summary

In this lesson, you learned how to request, provide, and manage professional recommendations on LinkedIn. In the next lesson, you learn to network with others on LinkedIn groups.

Participating in LinkedIn Groups

In this lesson, you learn how to participate in LinkedIn groups, manage your groups, and create your own group.

Understanding LinkedIn Groups

LinkedIn groups offer a way for like-minded individuals to share and discuss relevant topics related to the focus of the group. With LinkedIn groups, you can network and share ideas with industry peers, discover job leads and recruit quality talent, promote your career or business, and learn about a wide range of professional topics.

LinkedIn groups take many forms. There are groups for alumni, associations, nonprofits, professional interests, corporations, general networking, conference attendees, and personal interests. Your group activity appears on the home pages of your connections, providing additional visibility for your group actions and your groups.

LinkedIn imposes a limit of 50 group memberships per account holder. If you reach 50 groups and want to join another, you need to leave a group of which you're currently a member. Because of this limit, it's important to consider carefully which groups will provide you with the most value and help you meet your goals.

> PLAIN ENGLISH: **Open Groups Versus Members-Only Groups**
> LinkedIn offers two types of groups: open and members-only. An
> open group allows all LinkedIn users to view its Discussions tab as
> well as comment on and like its posts. You must join, however, to
> start your own discussions. Open groups are also indexed by
> search engines and allow people to share group content on
> Facebook and Twitter. A members-only group requires approval of
> the group owner to join and its content is private and can't be
> shared outside LinkedIn.

Joining a Group

One of the best ways to find a group to join is to search LinkedIn's Groups
Directory. To search the directory for potential groups, follow these steps:

1. On the global navigation bar, select **Groups Directory** from the
   Groups drop-down menu. The Featured Groups page opens,
   shown in Figure 11.1.

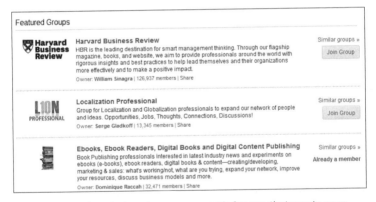

FIGURE 11.1   Join a featured group or search for one that meets your
criteria.

TIP: **Let LinkedIn Suggest Groups for You**

Another way to find good groups is to let LinkedIn suggest groups for you. To view a list of groups LinkedIn suggests based on your profile content, select **Groups You May Like** from the Groups menu on the global navigation bar.

2. In the Search Groups box, enter keywords related to the group you want to find. For example, you could enter the name of a company, school, professional association, skill, or hobby.

3. If you want to narrow your search results by category, select a category from the All Categories drop-down list. Options include groups for professional association members, alumni, corporate employees, conference attendees, nonprofits, and general networking.

4. If you want to narrow your search by language, select a language from the Choose drop-down list.

5. Click the **Search** button to open the Search Results page, which displays a preview of each group that matches your search criteria. The preview boxes include a group description, the group owner's name, and the number of members.

TIP: **Learn More About a Group Before You Join**

If you want to learn more about a group before joining, click the group title to view more details. For open groups, LinkedIn takes you to that group's Discussions tab. For members-only groups, LinkedIn opens a page with more group information including a list of people in your network who already belong to this group. If you want to join a members-only group, be sure to verify whether there are any requirements for membership. Some groups, for example, require you to be an alumnus of a school or company or a paid member of a professional association.

6. Click the **Join Group** button on the Search Results page.

What happens next depends on whether your target group is open or for members only:

▶ If the group is an open group, LinkedIn takes you directly to the group you joined. Click the **Here** link to open the Settings page where you can specify how you want to interact with the group. If the group was previously closed, LinkedIn displays a pop-up box informing you of this. See "Managing Group Settings" later in this lesson for more information.

▶ If the group is a members-only group, LinkedIn sends the group owner your request. To view your status, select **Your Groups** from the Groups menu on the global navigation bar. Your status for a new group on the Your Groups page is listed as *pending approval* (see Figure 11.2). This status remains until the group owner approves you. If you want to follow up with the group owner about a join request, click the **Send Message** link. If want to cancel your request to join the group, click the **Withdraw Request** link.

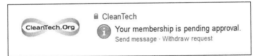

FIGURE 11.2   You need to await approval to access a members-only group.

Participating in Group Discussions

Participating in discussions is one of the greatest values of joining a group. With LinkedIn group discussions, you can view discussion threads for relevant professional information, add a comment to a current discussion, start your own discussion, or share news and links with group members.

> CAUTION: **Focus on Quality, Professional Discussions**
>
> As with everything else on LinkedIn, focus on intelligent, meaningful comments that add value to a discussion. Don't post a sales pitch or irrelevant comment just to lead people to your profile.

To view discussions for a group you belong to, click the **Groups** link on the global navigation menu to open the Your Groups page. From there, click the title of the group you want to view. Near the top of the Discussions tab, the discussions carousel (see Figure 11.3) rotates new discussion content every few seconds. This is a great way to preview what's new with your group.

FIGURE 11.3   Preview a rotating carousel of new discussion content.

Below each carousel item, you'll find links that enable you to like the discussion (similar to Facebook's Like feature), add a comment, or flag the post as promotional, job-related, or inappropriate. To view a discussion item in more detail, click its headline. The most popular discussions display below the carousel. Again, click a discussion item's headline to view the entire discussion, like it, add comments, follow it, flag it, or reply privately to the author.

Optionally, you can select **Latest Discussions** from the Choose Your View drop-down list to hide the carousel and display a list of the most recent discussions.

Liking a Discussion

If you find a discussion item particularly useful and interesting, you can show your support by clicking the **Like** button below it in the discussion carousel or on its detail page (see Figure 11.4). Liking a discussion alerts other group members as well as your followers that you found the discussion worthwhile. If you change your mind or click this button by mistake, you can unlike the discussion.

| | ◁ | 🖒 Like | ⬭ Comment | ⚑ Flag ▾ | More | ▷ |

FIGURE 11.4   Click the Like button to point out quality discussions to your fellow group members.

Adding Comments to a Discussion

To add a comment to a discussion, follow these steps:

1. Click the **Comment** button below any discussion item in the carousel. Alternatively, click the discussion headline to open it fully and comment on that page.

2. Enter your own comment in the text box, shown in Figure 11.5.

FIGURE 11.5   Contributing your own thoughts to a discussion.

3. If you want to receive email notification of any new comments in this discussion, select the **Send Me an Email for Each New Comment** check box.

4. Click the **Add Comment** button to post your comment.

TIP: **Reply Privately If You Don't Want to Post a Comment**

To reply privately to the original poster or anyone who posted a comment, select **Reply Privately** from the More drop-down menu.

After you post a comment, LinkedIn gives you 15 minutes to revise it. Click the **Edit Comment** link below your comment to make any changes. Click the **Delete** link to remove your comment from the discussion at any time.

Following Group Discussions and Members

If you want to know when someone adds a new comment to a discussion item you find particularly relevant, you can follow the discussion. To do so, click the discussion item's headline and click the **Follow** button below the discussion text on the detail page. LinkedIn sends you an email anytime someone adds a comment. By default, you follow any discussion that you start or comment on unless you specify that you don't want to receive email notification. If you decide you no longer want to follow a discussion, click the **Unfollow** button below it.

You can also manage your group-following activity by selecting **Your Activity** from the More menu at the top of the group. On the left side of the page, click the **Discussions You're Following** link to open a page with the same name.

To follow a group member, click the **Follow [First Name]** link below that person's photo. You can unfollow people by clicking the **Stop Following** link below their name or by going to the Discussions You're Following page.

Sharing a Discussion

Sharing discussion items on other social sites such as Facebook, Twitter, or Google+ is a good way to gain visibility for open groups. When you view the detail page for any discussion item in an open group, the Share Discussion box displays in the upper-right corner (see Figure 11.6).

FIGURE 11.6   Share a discussion post on your favorite social sites.

Starting a Discussion

On the Discussions tab, you can start your own discussion or share relevant links with other group members.

To start your own discussion, follow these steps:

1. Enter up to 200 characters in the Start a Discussion box at the top of the Discussions tab (to the right of your photo), shown in Figure 11.7. This text serves as your discussion headline, so consider carefully what you want to enter.

2. The section expands to include a second text box where you can add more details (up to 4,000 characters).

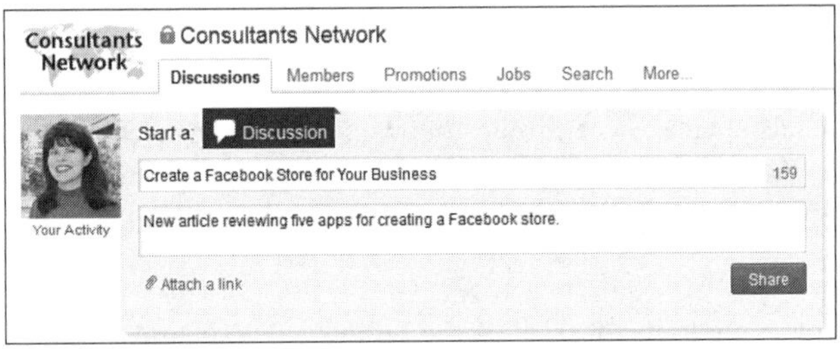

FIGURE 11.7   Start a discussion or share some news.

3. If you want to refer to an external URL, click the **Attach a Link** link. If not, skip to step 10.

4. Enter the URL you want to include in the Add a Link box, such as http://www.quepublishing.com. For example, you could attach a link to an article you just read in a major newspaper, or you could submit a great post from your favorite blog.

CAUTION: **Don't Overdo Self-Promotion**

Submitting your own articles, blog posts, or media coverage is acceptable, but don't overdo this feature as a promotional tool. Submit only the most informative, meaningful content that offers value to the members of your group. If your post is promotional, click the **Promotions** tab to post a promotion to your group.

---

5. Click the **Attach** button. LinkedIn searches for this URL and displays a title, description, and photo from this content it finds on this page (see Figure 11.8).

6. Optionally, click the **Edit** link to make changes to this default content.

7. Enter any changes to the title or description in the text boxes.

8. The Include Photo check box is selected by default, but you can remove this check mark if you don't want to include a photo. To change from the default photo, click the arrows below the photo to view alternative selections. LinkedIn searches for any photos on the page you're sharing and offers them as options.

FIGURE 11.8   Attach links to relevant external sites, such as a website, blog, or news site.

9. Click the **Save** button to save your edits.

10. Click the **Share** button to post your discussion item for your fellow group members to see.

Using a Group's Jobs Tab

A group's Jobs tab enables you to view and search LinkedIn job postings shared by other group members as well as post job-related discussion items.

On the Jobs tab, you can do the following:

▶ Click the **Jobs** link (selected by default) to view and search LinkedIn job postings shared by other group members (see Figure 11.9). To view the actual job posting, click its title.

▶ Click the **Job Discussions** tab to view job-related discussions posted by group members. To view the discussion, click its headline.

▶ Click the **Post a Job Discussion** link to open the Start a Job Discussion box. This box is nearly identical to the Start a Discussion box, described in the "Starting a Discussion" section earlier in this lesson.

FIGURE 11.9   View and search jobs related to your group.

> TIP: **Consider LinkedIn's Other Job Search and Recruiting Tools**
>
> For more ways to search for and post jobs on LinkedIn, click the **Jobs** link on the top navigation menu. Refer to Lesson 9, "Finding a Job," and Lesson 16, "Recruiting Job Candidates," for more information.

Managing Your Groups

LinkedIn offers you lots of flexibility in how you participate in, manage, and view the groups you join. You can also search for and share specific group information, and leave a group any time you want.

Viewing Your Groups

You can view a list of the groups you belong to by clicking the **Groups** link on the global navigation bar. The Your Groups page opens, shown in Figure 11.10.

FIGURE 11.10   View information about all your groups in one place.

A lock icon displays to the left of any group that is members-only. If this icon doesn't display, the group is an open group.

To go to a group's Discussions tab, click the title of the group. Depending on the activity of a group, several icons might display below its title on the Your Groups page. Pause your mouse over each icon to determine its function before clicking it. Possible icons include

▸ **Statistics for This Group**—View group statistics, such as its member demographics, growth, and activity.

▸ **[Number] New Discussions**—View new group discussions. The number of new discussions since your last visit displays in the upper-right corner of the icon.

▸ **[Number] Jobs and Job Discussions**—View new jobs and job discussions on the Jobs tab. The number of new items since your last visit displays in the upper-right corner of the icon.

▸ **[First Name's] Recent Activity**—View recent group activity from your connections.

TIP: **View Your Group Information on Your Profile**
You can also view a list of the groups you belong to on your profile.

Changing the Display Order of Your Groups

For easy access to your groups, LinkedIn displays the first three groups on the Your Groups page on the Groups menu you access from the global navigation bar (see Figure 11.11).

FIGURE 11.11   Access your favorite groups directly from your home page.

If you're a frequent participant in group activity, it's a good idea to display your favorite groups on this navigation menu. You can also increase the number of displayed groups from 3 to as many as 10.

To change the display order of your groups, follow these steps:

1. On the global navigation bar, click the **Groups** link.

2. On the Your Groups page, click the **Reorder** link. The Groups Order and Display page opens, shown in Figure 11.12.

Groups Order and Display	
Choose which groups display in what order in the main navigation.	

Groups (49)

Display the first 3 ▼ groups in the navigation. (Pending groups will not show up)

Order		Group Name
1		Book Publishing Professionals
2	⌅	Women 2.0
3	⌅	Social Media Today
4	⌅	Consultants Network

FIGURE 11.12   Choosing the order in which your groups appear.

3. Select the number of group links to display on the Groups drop-down menu on the global navigation bar. Options range from 1 to 10.

4. Use the Order field to move each of your groups up or down until you reach your desired display order.

> NOTE: **Change Your Settings for Each of Your Groups**
> You can specify different settings for each of your groups. Click the **Member Settings** link to make changes to a particular group. See "Managing Group Settings" later in this lesson for more information.

5. Click the **Save Changes** button at the bottom of the page to save your changes.

Viewing Group Members

To view a list of group members, click the **Members** tab on any group page. This page tells you how many members a group has and displays previews of each group member, starting with you. From there, LinkedIn lists your 1st degree connections, your 2nd degree connections, and, finally, all other members.

Depending on members' settings and connection to you, their preview could include a photo, a profile link, a professional headline, their number of connections, and links to connect and send a message.

To search a group's member list for members matching specific criteria, enter keywords in the Search Members box and click the **Search** button. You can also search groups using the Search tab or from the quick search box on the top navigation menu. Refer to Lesson 7, "Searching on LinkedIn," for more information on searching for people.

Viewing Group Updates

To view the latest group updates, select **Updates** from the More menu on any group page. The Updates page lists activity for the current and previous day, such as who joined the group, who started a discussion, who posted comments, and so forth. The default view is All Updates. Click the **People You're Following** tab to display updates only from those group members you follow.

Managing Group Settings

To revise your settings for a group, select **Your Settings** from the More menu on any group page. The Settings page opens (see Figure 11.13), which gives you the option to modify the visibility and contact options for a specific group.

```
Settings

  Visibility Settings
  Group Logo:              ☑ Display the group logo on your profile.
  Contact Settings
  Contact Email:           Select the email address to use when receiving communications from the group.
                           patrice@patricerutledge.com  ▾    Add a new email address »
  Activity:                ☐ Send me an email for each new discussion.
  Digest Email:            ☐ Send me a digest of all activity in this group.
                             Note: Your email address will remain hidden from members of this group.
  Announcements:           ☐ Allow the group manager to send me an email (no more than once a week).
  Member Messages:         ☑ Allow members of this group to send me messages via LinkedIn.
  Updates Settings
  Updates:                 To change settings for group Network Updates, go to your Account Settings.

            [ Save Changes ]  or Cancel
```

FIGURE 11.13   Specify how you want to connect with your group.

On this page, you can choose to

▸ Display a group logo on your profile.

▸ Select the email address where you want to receive group communications.

▸ Have LinkedIn send you an email for each new discussion.

▸ Have LinkedIn send you a daily or weekly digest of all group activity.

▸ Allow the group owner to send you an email.

▶ Allow members of this group to send you messages via LinkedIn. (They won't see your personal email address.)

> NOTE: **View Group Updates Online**
>
> Even if you don't want to receive email notifications, you can keep up with your groups on LinkedIn. Your home page displays group updates, and the Updates page for each group summarizes the latest activity as well.

Sharing a Group with Other LinkedIn Users

If you're a member of a particular group that you think your connections would also enjoy, let them know about it by clicking the **Share Group** link on the Discussions tab of any group. From there, you can click the Share on LinkedIn link to open the Share dialog box, which enables you to post an update, post to other groups, or send a message to one or more of your connections.

Refer to Lesson 6, "Communicating with Other LinkedIn Members," for more information about the inbox and sending messages.

Leaving a Group

If you decide that a group no longer meets your needs or you have to pare down your current group membership to make room for new groups, you can easily leave a group.

To do so, select Your Settings from the **More** menu on any group page and then click the **Leave Group** button. LinkedIn removes you from the group.

Creating and Managing Your Own Group

Creating your own group is a good way to develop a community for a topic, profession, or interest. Before you create a group, consider the following:

▶ Is there already a similar group on LinkedIn Groups? If so, how will your group differ? What value will you add?

▶ Is your proposed group an advertisement in disguise? Although many LinkedIn members do benefit from their participation with LinkedIn groups, you need to create a group whose focus is providing value and community to its members. If you don't, your group most likely won't succeed.

▶ Do you have the time to maintain and support your group? If you don't respond quickly to join requests and keep the activity going with your group, it won't flourish.

Creating Your Own Group

To create a new LinkedIn group, follow these steps:

1. Select **Create a Group** from the Groups menu on the global navigation bar. The Create a Group page opens, shown in Figure 11.14.

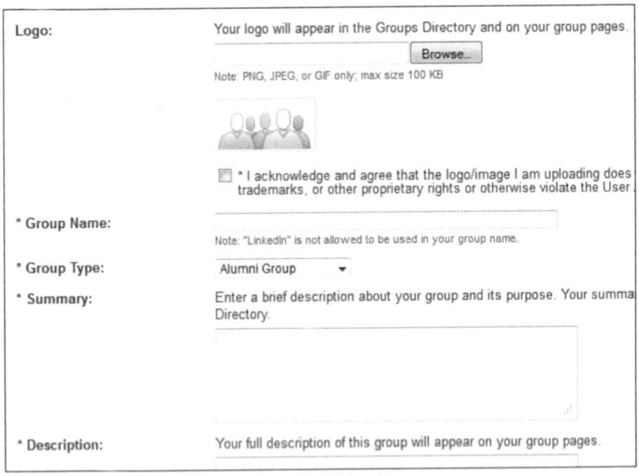

Logo:	Your logo will appear in the Groups Directory and on your group pages.
	[Browse..]
	Note: PNG, JPEG, or GIF only; max size 100 KB
	☐ * I acknowledge and agree that the logo/image I am uploading does trademarks, or other proprietary rights or otherwise violate the User
* Group Name:	
	Note: "LinkedIn" is not allowed to be used in your group name.
* Group Type:	Alumni Group ▼
* Summary:	Enter a brief description about your group and its purpose. Your summa Directory.
* Description:	Your full description of this group will appear on your group pages.

FIGURE 11.14   Creating your own group.

2. Click the **Browse** button in the Logo section to select and upload a logo for your group. Supported formats include PNG, JPEG, and GIF files no larger than 100KB. Select the check box below your logo to confirm that you have legal right to use this image.

3. Enter a group name. If your group also exists outside of LinkedIn, you can increase visibility by including the actual group name rather than just an acronym. For example, enter International Association of Business Communicators (IABC) instead of only IABC.

4. Select a group type. Options include alumni, corporate, conference, networking, nonprofit, professional, or other groups. The Other group type is most appropriate for special interest or hobby groups that don't fit into any other category.

5. Enter a summary of your group. In this text box, indicate your group's focus, goals, and any membership benefits your group might provide for LinkedIn members. This summary appears in the Groups Directory.

6. In the Description text box, enter more details to display on your group pages.

7. If your group has an external website, enter the URL in the Website field.

8. Enter the group owner email. LinkedIn sends all messages about your group to this email address.

9. If you want to approve new group members automatically, select the **Auto-Join** option button.

10. If you want to approve group membership requests manually, select the **Request to Join** option button. This option is selected by default. LinkedIn sends a message whenever someone requests to join your group, and you must approve the request manually. This requires extra effort on your part, but it ensures that only qualified people join your group. If your group members work for the same organization, you can pre-approve members with a specific email domain.

11. Select the **Display This Group in the Groups Directory** check box or the **Allow Group Members to Display the Logo on Their Profiles** check box if you want to enable these options. These are great promotional tools for your group. Unless you have a specific need for privacy, it's a good idea to make your group visible.

12. Select a language for your group. English is the default language for groups, but LinkedIn offers numerous language choices.

13. If your group is for members who are located in a specific geographic location, select the **Location** check box. The Country and Postal Code fields appear so that you can specify the exact location of your group.

14. If you want to announce your new group on Twitter, select the **Twitter Announcement** check box. LinkedIn sends an announcement from your linked Twitter account.

15. If you agree to the Terms of Service, select the check box. The Terms of Service cover your rights to provide LinkedIn with the email addresses of group members and LinkedIn's rights to use the logo you upload.

16. Click either the **Create an Open Group** button or the **Create a Members-Only Group** button to create your group. For more information about the differences between open and members-only groups, click the **Learn About Open Groups** button or refer to the "Understanding LinkedIn Groups" section earlier in this lesson.

LinkedIn reviews your request to create a new group and approves the group if it meets LinkedIn's guidelines.

Managing Your Own Group

After LinkedIn approves your group, you can start inviting and accepting members.

As a reminder, click the **Groups** link on the global navigation bar to open the Your Groups page where you can access all your LinkedIn groups. To manage your group, select the **Manage** tab on your group's page.

On the Manage tab, you can

▶ Approve or reject requests to join your group.

▶ Send invitations to LinkedIn members asking them to join your group.

▶ Upload a pre-approved list of email addresses for your group in the CSV format. This option is useful if your group also exists outside of LinkedIn, and you know the members you want to pre-approve.

TIP: **Create Your CSV File in Microsoft Excel**

Enter your list of pre-approved members in an Excel file with columns for first name, last name, and email. Save your spreadsheet as a CSV file. CSV stands for *comma-separated values*, a common text file format.

Summary

In this lesson, you learned how to join and participate in LinkedIn groups, create your own groups, and manage your own groups. Next, learn how to maximize your visibility and demonstrate expertise using LinkedIn Answers.

LESSON 12

Using LinkedIn Answers

In this lesson, you learn how to ask and answer questions that give you valuable feedback from the LinkedIn community and develop your reputation as an expert in your field.

Understanding LinkedIn Answers

LinkedIn Answers is an interactive feature that enables you to ask questions, receive input from a worldwide network of peers and experts, share your own expertise, and develop your platform as an expert.

CAUTION: LinkedIn Answers Is for Professional Discussion, Not Promotion

Understand that LinkedIn Answers is for genuine information sharing among professional peers. It's not the place for sales pitches (overt or disguised), open requests for help in getting a job, and so forth. That said, asking intelligent, relevant questions and providing useful answers with real value can help develop your expert image on LinkedIn.

To view questions and answers, select **Answers** from the More drop-down menu on the global navigation bar. The Answers page opens, shown in Figure 12.1.

On the Answers Home tab, you can view the following:

▶ A box with shortcuts for asking and answering questions. LinkedIn recommends up to five categories based on previous questions you've answered. If you haven't answered questions, this section displays the Answer Now button.

FIGURE 12.1 Participate in the LinkedIn community by asking and answering questions.

▶ A list of recent questions from your network.

▶ The week's top experts, based on the number of questions they've answered and the number of times their answers have been selected as best answers.

▶ The My Q&A box listing your open questions, if any.

▶ A complete list of LinkedIn Answers categories.

▶ Links to questions in languages other than English.

You can ask and answer questions that relate to professional topics in more than 20 categories, including Management, Marketing and Sales, Professional Development, Finance and Accounting, Technology, and more.

Your activity on LinkedIn Answers also appears in the Q & A box on your profile, shown in Figure 12.2.

> **Patrice-Anne Rutledge's Q & A**
>
> Expertise in
>
> • Writing and Editing (2 best answers)
> • Freelancing and Contracting (1 best answer)
> • Occupational Training (1 best answer)
>
> 6 Questions - 8 Answers   See all Q&A »

FIGURE 12.2 Your profile promotes your activity on LinkedIn Answers.

This box lists your questions, answers, and expertise. If you've received any best-answer votes, a green square with a white star appears in this box. To remove the Q & A box from your profile, click the **Change This Setting** link. For example, if you answer questions that don't relate to your professional experience, you might not want to display these on your profile.

Asking a Question

Asking a question is a good way to get input from LinkedIn's hundreds of millions of members worldwide. It's also a good way to demonstrate your own expertise. Remember, however, to avoid asking questions related to a personal job search, recruiting for a specific job opening, or promoting your business.

To ask a question:

1. Select **Answers** from the More drop-down menu on the global navigation bar.

2. Click the **Ask a Question** tab to open the Ask a Question page, shown in Figure 12.3.

FIGURE 12.3 Ask a question to tap into the insight of LinkedIn's millions of members.

> TIP: **Take a Shortcut in Asking a Question**
> You can also ask your question in the Ask a Question box on the LinkedIn Answers Home tab. When you click **Next**, LinkedIn takes you to the Ask a Question tab where you can complete your question.

3. In the first text box, enter a one-line question. Make sure your question is clear and concise. Vague, open-ended questions rarely receive good feedback. For example, asking LinkedIn members for suggestions on online invoicing applications suited to a small business is a good, focused question. Asking members how to make lots of money with your new website, which you promote in the details section, is not the way to use LinkedIn Answers.

4. If you want to send your question only to specific people (up to 200 of your connections), select the **Only Share This Question with Connections I Select** check box. For maximum response and visibility, it's best to post your question to the public LinkedIn Answers section.

5. In the Add Details box, provide pertinent background information to clarify your question further. Be careful, however, of adding too much detail. Although you can add content up to 2,000 characters, many people skip over lengthy questions.

6. Categorize your question based on the available categories and subcategories. You can add a second category if desired.

7. If your question is location-specific, select the **My Question Is Focused Around a Specific Geographic Location** check box. LinkedIn asks you to select a country and postal code, if applicable.

8. Specify whether your question relates to one of the following: recruiting, promoting your services, or job seeking.

9. Click the **Ask Question** button to post your question.

NOTE: **Alternatives to LinkedIn Answers**

If your question relates to recruiting, promotion, or a job search, LinkedIn offers links to other features that might be more appropriate than LinkedIn Answers. For example, consider posting a job using LinkedIn Jobs or promoting your services on a LinkedIn Company Page instead.

LinkedIn's millions of members now have the opportunity to view and answer your question, providing valuable feedback and information.

LinkedIn automatically closes your question in seven days, but offers you the choice to extend the question another week or close it manually before seven days. See the section "Viewing and Modifying Your Questions and Answers" later in this lesson for more information.

One final step is to select a best answer to the question you posted, if you feel one response provided the most value. LinkedIn members who receive the best answer designations are recognized in the LinkedIn Answers list of experts and on their profiles.

Browsing Open Questions to Answer

In addition to viewing questions to answer on the Answers Home tab, you can find more questions on the Answer Questions tab. When you select this tab, the Browse Open Questions page opens. Question summaries appear in the order of their author's connection to you. For example, questions from your 1st degree connections appear first, and so forth. Click the **Date** link to sort questions by date instead.

TIP: **Answer Questions in LinkedIn's Recommended Categories**

On the Answers Home tab, LinkedIn recommends question categories for you based on your profile and any questions you've previously answered.

Figure 12.4 shows a sample question summary.

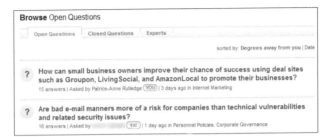

Browse Open Questions

| Open Questions | Closed Questions | Experts |

sorted by: Degrees away from you | Date

? How can small business owners improve their chance of success using deal sites such as Groupon, LivingSocial, and AmazonLocal to promote their businesses?
15 answers | Asked by Patrice-Anne Rutledge (YOU) | 3 days ago in Internet Marketing

? Are bad e-mail manners more of a risk for companies than technical vulnerabilities and related security issues?
16 answers | Asked by [illegible] (1st) | 1 day ago in Personnel Policies, Corporate Governance

FIGURE 12.4   To elicit the best responses, ask clear, concise questions.

In addition to the question title, LinkedIn displays the number of answers the question has received, its author, the date it was posted, and its categories.

To browse questions relating to a specific category, click one of the links in the Browse box on the right side of your screen. Most categories have subcategories you can use to narrow the subject matter of posted questions.

> TIP: **Subscribe to an RSS Feed to Stay Informed**
>
> If you're interested in questions related to a specific category, you can subscribe to the RSS feed for that category by clicking the link next to the orange and white feed icon at the bottom of the Browse box. LinkedIn opens the Subscribe Now pop-up box, which enables you to subscribe using your favorite feed reader (such as My Yahoo! or Google Reader). Refer to Lesson 4, "Customizing Your LinkedIn Settings," for more information about subscribing to RSS feeds.

You can also browse questions in a specific language. LinkedIn enables members to post questions in more than a dozen languages.

Finally, the Browse Open Questions page also offers links for viewing closed questions and popular experts.

> **NOTE: Reporting Problem Questions**
>
> If you view a question that you feel is inappropriate, click the **Report Question As** link on its detail page to alert LinkedIn staff. Potential reasons for reporting a question include duplicate questions, open advertising, recruitment messages, inappropriate content, connection-building spam, or misrepresentation.

Answering Questions

To post a public reply to a question, follow these steps:

1. Click the question title link to view the question's details. Figure 12.5 illustrates a sample question.

FIGURE 12.5   You can answer questions publicly or privately.

2. Click the **Answer** button to expand the Your Answer box, shown in Figure 12.6.

3. Enter your answer in the text box. Remember to provide value and true information. Don't sell your own expertise and services. Let your LinkedIn profile do that for you.

4. Optionally, list up to three web resources. Include the complete URL, such as http://www.patricerutledge.com.

5. Optionally, click the **Select Experts** button to open your connection list. You can choose up to three experts from your network to recommend for this question. The experts you suggest appear in your answer with links to their profiles.

FIGURE 12.6   You can include up to three web links with your answer.

6. Enter an optional, private note to the person who posted the question. No other LinkedIn members will see this content.

7. Enter the characters that display in the text box (if one displays) to verify that you're a real person answering a question.

8. Click **Submit** to post your answer.

If you don't want to answer a question directly, you can

▶ Click the **Reply Privately** link to send a private message to the person who posted the question.

▶ Click the **Share This** link to email this question to others or post to the social bookmarking site Delicious. This is a good way to expand the visibility of LinkedIn questions.

When you answer a question, it's important to provide an intelligent, helpful response. Responding to numerous questions with vague answers in an effort to increase your visibility won't pay off in the long run. Focus on quality rather than quantity and answer only when you have something meaningful to contribute.

LinkedIn members who post questions can award a best-answer designation to the person who provides the most helpful answer. When you receive Best Answer votes, you increase your ranking on the list of experts.

Searching LinkedIn Answers by Keyword

LinkedIn's advanced search functionality lets you search its vast collection of questions and answers for specific information.

Searching by keyword enables you to:

- ▶ Find specific questions to answer

- ▶ Discover solutions to your own professional questions from LinkedIn's large collection of information

- ▶ Determine what people are asking and saying about you, your company, or your products

- ▶ Collect competitive intelligence

To search by keyword:

1. Click the **Advanced Answers Search** tab on the Answers page. Figure 12.7 shows your search possibilities.

2. In the Keywords field, enter your search terms. The more specific your keywords, the more targeted your results will be.

TIP: **Take Advantage of Advanced Search Techniques**

To search on a specific phrase, use quotation marks (such as "social media" to search specifically for social media). Refer to Lesson 7, "Searching on LinkedIn," for more information about advanced searching techniques.

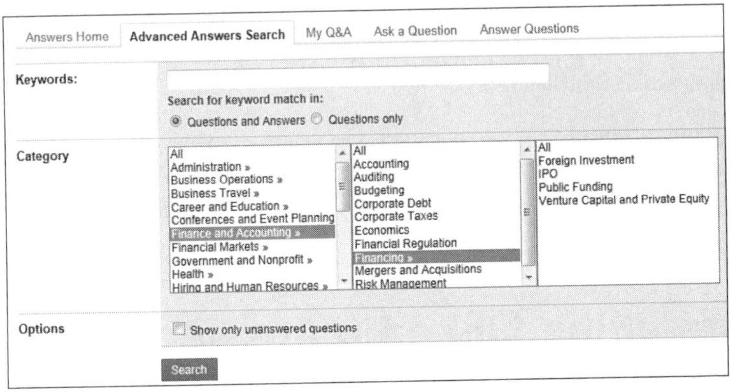

FIGURE 12.7   Search LinkedIn Answers for specific keywords.

3. Specify whether you want to search questions and answers or questions only.

4. Select a category and related subcategory in the Category field.

5. If you want to view only questions that haven't been answered, select the **Show Only Unanswered Questions** check box.

6. Click the **Search** button to display search results.

To view only open questions, click the **Open Questions** tab. From this page, you can also further refine your search criteria if necessary.

TIP: **Search LinkedIn Answers from the Quick Search Box**

You can also search LinkedIn Answers from the quick search box on the global navigation bar. Select **Answers** from the drop-down list, enter your keywords, and click the **Search** button. Or click the **Advanced** link to open the Advanced Answers Search tab.

Viewing and Modifying Your Questions and Answers

To view and modify your own activity on LinkedIn Answers, click the **My Q&A** tab on the Answers page.

On the first tab, My Questions, LinkedIn displays a summary of the questions you've asked. Click the link of any question to view it; if the question is still open, you can revise it. Figure 12.8 shows a sample open question.

Go back to My Questions | Next »

Your question closes in **7 days**:
* Forward this question

Close Question Now

How can small business owners improve their chance of success using deal sites such as Groupon, LivingSocial, and AmazonLocal to promote their businesses?

Specifically, how can they convert a deal customer into a long-term customer?

posted 8 minutes ago in Internet Marketing | Clarify my question

Share This ▾

FIGURE 12.8   You can modify a question that's still open.

If the question is still open, you can

▶ Click the **Forward This Question** link to send the question to up to 200 of your connections.

▶ Click the **Close Question Now** button to close the question before it closes automatically in seven days. You can also hide your closed question from public view. For maximum visibility, it's best to keep your question open and allow it to remain on LinkedIn Answers. If you make a mistake or no longer want to display your question, however, you can close and hide it.

▶ Click the **Clarify My Question** link, below the question itself, to open the Clarify Your Question page and add related details. LinkedIn doesn't allow you to edit the question you posted.

▶ Click the **Share This** link to share your question by email or on the social bookmarking site Delicious.

On the second tab, My Answers, LinkedIn displays summaries of all the questions you've answered. The right side of this page lists the categories in which you've demonstrated expertise (based on receiving "best answer" ratings), your answer ratings for closed questions, and statistics about your activity on LinkedIn Answers.

You can modify or delete your answers to open questions only. Click the **Clarify My Answer** link to add clarification to your existing answer. Click the **Delete My Answer** link to delete your answer.

Summary

In this lesson, you learned how to maximize the potential of LinkedIn Answers for finding professional solutions, demonstrating your expertise, and interacting with a worldwide audience of millions. Next, learn to add more content to your profile with LinkedIn applications.

Using LinkedIn Applications

In this lesson, you learn how to enhance your LinkedIn experience with LinkedIn applications, including how to add, manage, and remove applications.

Understanding LinkedIn Applications

LinkedIn applications are optional extensions to LinkedIn that enhance the content and effectiveness of your profile, foster collaboration with your network, and integrate your LinkedIn data with other sites to provide further research and competitive intelligence opportunities.

The following LinkedIn applications are currently available, with more in development:

- Blog Link by SixApart
- Box.net Files by Box.net
- Events by LinkedIn
- E-Bookshelf by FT Press
- GitHub by LinkedIn
- Google Presentations by Google
- Lawyer Ratings by LexisNexis Martindale-Hubbell
- Legal Updates by JD Supra

- ▶ My Travel by TripIt

- ▶ Polls by LinkedIn

- ▶ Portfolio Display by Behance

- ▶ Projects and Teamspaces by Manymoon

- ▶ Reading List by Amazon

- ▶ Real Estate Pro by Rofo

- ▶ SlideShare Presentations by SlideShare

- ▶ WordPress by WordPress

All LinkedIn applications are free, but some require you to have an account with an application that might charge fees based on your usage. For example, Box.net Files offer both free and fee-based plans.

Choosing the Right Applications

LinkedIn applications offer many options for sharing and collaborating. At times, the number of choices is overwhelming. Although some applications, such as My Travel and Real Estate Pro, are unique in terms of the features they provide, other applications overlap in their functionality. For example, both Blog Link and WordPress enable you to share blog posts on your profile. You can share presentations using Google Presentations, SlideShare Presentations, and even Box.net Files.

Here are some tips for making the most of LinkedIn applications:

- ▶ Analyze how each application fits into your strategic plan and helps you meet your goals. Just because something sounds interesting doesn't make it worthwhile to add.

- ▶ If more than one application performs the same function, compare their features before you pick one to use. Fortunately, LinkedIn applications are easy to add and remove.

- ▶ Focus on quality rather than quantity when choosing the documents and presentations you would like to share. A resume, portfolio, or presentation that highlights your business can enhance the effectiveness and reach of your LinkedIn profile, but don't add so many documents that the important ones are lost in the mix.

▶ Consider your personal privacy with all the documents and data you share online. For example, adding your resume to your profile can aid in your job search, but you might not want to include your home address or phone number.

▶ Determine whether you have the legal right to post presentations or other documents you created for an employer.

Adding Applications

To add an application to your profile or home page, follow these steps:

1. On the global navigation bar, select **Get More Applications** from the More drop-down list. The Applications page opens (see Figure 13.1).

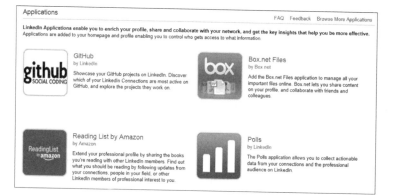

FIGURE 13.1 Enhance your LinkedIn experience with one of the many available applications.

2. Select the application you want to add. The page for that application opens. Figure 13.2 illustrates the SlideShare Presentations page, as an example.

FIGURE 13.2   SlideShare Presentations is one of many LinkedIn applications.

3. The Application Info box appears on the right side of every application page. In this box, choose whether you want to display the application on your profile, on your LinkedIn home page, or on both.

4. Click the **Add Application** button to add the application and enter details specific to that application.

The rest of this section explains how to set up individual applications. This lesson provides detailed instructions for only the most popular applications, not every available application.

When you add an application, a link to it appears on the More drop-down menu on the global navigation bar. If you haven't added any applications, only the Reading List by Amazon, Events, and Polls links appear by default.

Adding the Blog Link Application

The Blog Link application enables you to post summaries of your blog posts to your LinkedIn profile. You can also follow the blog posts of

LinkedIn members in your network. Blog Link supports blogs on multiple platforms including TypePad, Movable Type, Vox, Wordpress.com, Wordpress.org, Blogger, LiveJournal, and more.

> **NOTE: If You Use WordPress, Consider the WordPress Application**
>
> WordPress users have two choices for displaying their blog posts on their profiles: the Blog Link application and the WordPress application. Both applications serve the same function, but they display your blog posts in a different format. If you use WordPress, try both applications to see which one you prefer. See "Adding the WordPress Application" later in this lesson for more information.

Before adding the Blog Link application, verify that the URL to your blog appears in the Websites section on your profile. Refer to Lesson 2, "Creating Your Profile," for more information on listing your blog in this section. The application pulls your blog data from your profile and doesn't work properly if you don't have a listed blog.

To add the Blog Link application, follow the steps listed in "Adding Applications" earlier in this lesson, selecting the Blog Link application on the Applications page. The Blog Link application opens.

The Blog Link application searches for your blog posts and includes summaries on your LinkedIn profile (see Figure 13.3). They also appear on the By Me tab in the Blog Link application.

> **CAUTION: What to Do If Your Blog Posts Don't Appear on Your Profile**
>
> If your blog posts don't appear on your profile, verify that you selected the Display on My Profile check box on the initial application page. Also, verify that your blog is listed on the Websites section of your profile. The Blog Link application pulls its content from the blog listed in this section.

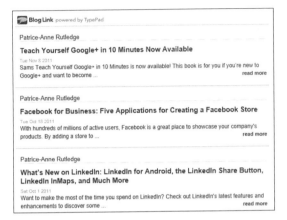

FIGURE 13.3   Automatically post your blog updates to your LinkedIn profile.

Blog Link also searches for blog posts from your connections and includes these on the From My Contacts tab. If you don't want to view a particular blog, click the **Hide This Feed** link below its title. Blog posts from other LinkedIn members don't appear on your profile.

CAUTION: **Only Add Blogs That Relate to Your Professional Activities**

Remember that your LinkedIn profile is part of your professional presence online. Include only blog content that supports your professional image. Personal blogs or blogs covering controversial topics might not be suitable to share with your LinkedIn connections.

Adding the Box.net Files Application

The Box.net Files application enables you to share content from Box.net (www.box.net), a leading online collaboration and file-sharing website. With this application, you can post files such as resumes, portfolios, and presentations to your profile, collaborate privately with your LinkedIn connections, and view and edit your files online.

To add the Box.net Files application, follow the steps listed in the "Adding Applications" section earlier in this lesson, selecting the Box.net Files application on the Applications page.

The Box.net Files application opens, requesting that you log in to your Box.net Files account or sign up for a free account.

After you log in, you can upload files, view your connections' public files, and collaborate privately with your connections.

The files you selected to display publicly on your profile appear in the Applications section, shown in Figure 13.4.

LinkedIn Profile		Menu	▼
📄 Chronological Resume.doc	03/27/09	71 KB
📄 Functional Resume.doc	03/02/09	53 KB
📄 Value Presentation.pdf	03/27/09	53 KB

FIGURE 13.4   Posting your resume can help you stand out from the crowd of other job seekers.

Adding the Reading List by Amazon Application

The Reading List by Amazon application enables you to share book recommendations and reading plans with your LinkedIn connections. LinkedIn installs the Reading List by Amazon application by default.

To add a book to your profile using the Reading List by Amazon application, follow these steps:

1. On the global navigation bar, select **Reading List by Amazon** on the More drop-down menu. The Reading List by Amazon application opens, with the Network Updates tab selected.

2. In the What Are You Reading section, enter the title of a book you would like to include on your profile.

3. Click the **Search Books** button to display possible matches. If the book you want to display doesn't appear, revise your search results or search according to author name.

4. Click the **Select** button below the matching title to continue to the next page (see Figure 13.5).

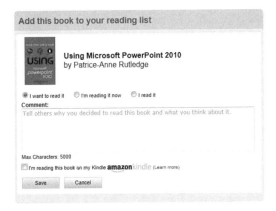

FIGURE 13.5   Share your reading recommendations with your network.

5. Select one of the following reading options: I Want to Read It, I'm Reading It Now, or I Read It.

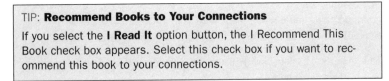

TIP: **Recommend Books to Your Connections**
If you select the **I Read It** option button, the I Recommend This Book check box appears. Select this check box if you want to recommend this book to your connections.

6. Enter a comment of up to 5,000 characters. In your comments, explain to your connections why you're including this book and the value it offers.

7. Select the **I'm Reading This Book on My Kindle** check box if you're reading the Kindle version.

8. Click the **Save** button to update your reading list.

The book now appears on your profile (see Figure 13.6) and home page (if you selected these display options).

FIGURE 13.6   Your connections can view your reading list on your profile.

In addition to the Network Updates tab, the Reading List by Amazon application also includes three other tabs:

▶ **Your Reading List**—Displays a list of all books you added to your reading list. You can edit or delete an existing entry from this list.

▶ **Industry Updates**—Displays books on the reading lists of others in your industry.

▶ **All Recent Updates**—Displays reading list updates from all LinkedIn members.

Adding the SlideShare Presentations Application

Using the SlideShare Presentations application, you can embed presentations and other documents from SlideShare (www.slideshare.net), the popular presentation-sharing site. If you don't have an account on SlideShare, you can sign up for one from LinkedIn and start uploading files. The files you choose appear on your profile (see Figure 13.7).

Although SlideShare is best known for sharing presentations such as PowerPoint files, you can also share files of up to 20MB in numerous formats, including Microsoft Word, Microsoft Excel, and PDF. You can also embed YouTube videos in your presentations to give your LinkedIn profile some added flair.

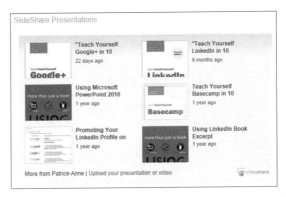

FIGURE 13.7   Use SlideShare to incorporate slideshows into your LinkedIn profile.

To add the SlideShare Presentations application, follow the steps listed in the "Adding Applications" section earlier in this lesson, selecting the SlideShare Presentations application on the Applications page. The SlideShare application opens.

Enter your username and password if you already have a SlideShare account and click the **Link Existing Profile** button. Alternatively, sign up for a SlideShare account and click the **Create New Profile** button.

The SlideShare application includes the following five tabs:

▶ **Home**—Displays the Network Activity list, detailing the presentations your connections have uploaded. Click the name of any presentation to view it in a player, tweet it on Twitter, share with your connections, add comments, or mark it as a favorite.

▶ **Explore**—Lists the most viewed and most recently uploaded presentations.

▶ **Your Connections**—Displays the presentations your connections have uploaded.

▶ **Your Slidespace**—Offers the following display options: Your Presentations, Your Favorites, or Your Connections. This tab also includes a link to the Settings page where you can specify whether you want to display presentation thumbnails or a complete presentation in a player.

▶ **Upload**—Enables you to upload files to LinkedIn.

Adding the WordPress Application

If you have a WordPress blog, you can display your blog posts on your LinkedIn profile. This application works with both self-hosted WordPress.org blogs and hosted WordPress.com blogs.

TIP: Also Consider the Blog Link Application

If you use a solution other than WordPress to host your blog, check out the Blog Link application instead. WordPress users can choose between adding the WordPress application or adding the Blog Link application. Each application performs the same function, but each displays posts in different formats. Refer to the "Adding the Blog Link Application" section earlier in this lesson for more information.

To add the WordPress application, follow these steps:

1. Follow the steps listed in the "Adding Applications" section earlier in this lesson, selecting the WordPress application on the Applications page. The WordPress application opens, shown in Figure 13.8.

FIGURE 13.8   Specify the URL of your WordPress blog.

2. Enter the complete URL of your blog in the text box, such as http://www.patricerutledge.com/blog.

3. Indicate whether you want to show all recent blog posts or only those tagged LinkedIn.

> TIP: **You Can Choose to Include Only Selected Blog Posts on LinkedIn**
>
> Tag your blog posts in WordPress with the "linkedin" tag to select which ones you want to appear on LinkedIn.

4. Click the **Save** button to preview your blog posts.

Your WordPress blog posts now appear on your profile and home page (if you selected these display options).

Working with LinkedIn Polls

The Polls application enables you to poll LinkedIn users about relevant professional topics and participate in polls other LinkedIn members create. A LinkedIn poll is a short question with the option of providing as many as five answers. Members select their preferred answers and the Polls application tallies the results.

LinkedIn installs the Polls application by default. To open the Polls app, select **Polls** from the More drop-down menu on the global navigation bar.

On the Polls page, you can do the following:

▶ Click the title of a poll to participate in it. You can submit your own poll vote, add a comment after you vote, view poll results, including voter demographics, or share the poll on your blog or other social site. Figure 13.9 shows a sample poll.

▶ Search for polls by keyword.

▶ Click the **Create a New Poll** button to create your own poll (see Figure 13.10). You can enter a question of up to 120 characters with up to five answers and, optionally, share on several social media sites.

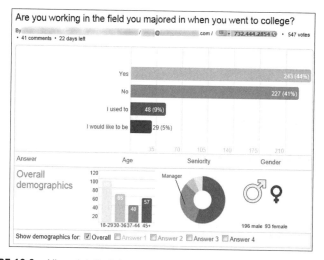

FIGURE 13.9   View detailed demographic information for each poll.

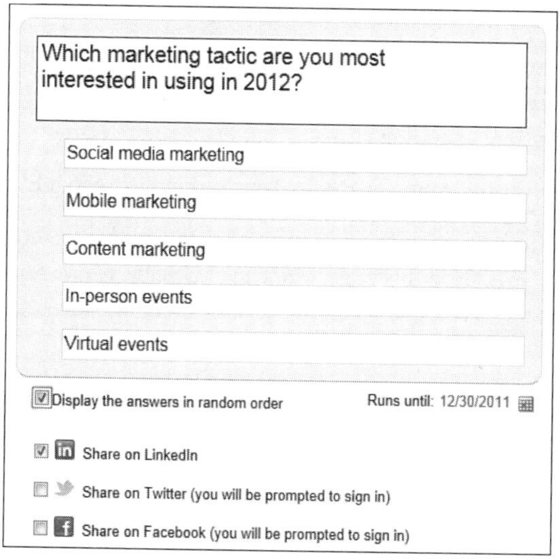

FIGURE 13.10   Use a LinkedIn poll to gain valuable insight and perform market research.

▶ Click the **Email Settings** button to specify how you want to be alerted to poll activity. You can receive an email when a poll you've created ends, a poll you've voted on ends, or someone comments after you on a poll.

Adding and Managing LinkedIn Events

The LinkedIn Events application enables you to add events to LinkedIn's events calendar, promote events to LinkedIn members, and find events you want to attend. LinkedIn focuses on professional events, both in-person and virtual, rather than personal events.

LinkedIn installs the Events application by default. To open the LinkedIn Events page, select **Events** from the More drop-down menu on the global navigation bar.

On the Events page, you can do the following:

▶ View a list of events you might be interested in. LinkedIn displays events related to your profession or those which your connections are attending.

▶ Search for upcoming events by keyword in the Search Events box.

▶ Click the title of an event to view its details page, as shown in Figure 13.11. On this page, you can announce your attendance, follow the event, add a comment, view other attendees, and share the event on your other social sites.

▶ Click the **Create an Event** button to post your own event on LinkedIn. The Create an Event on LinkedIn page, shown in Figure 13.12, walks you through the steps needed to create an event.

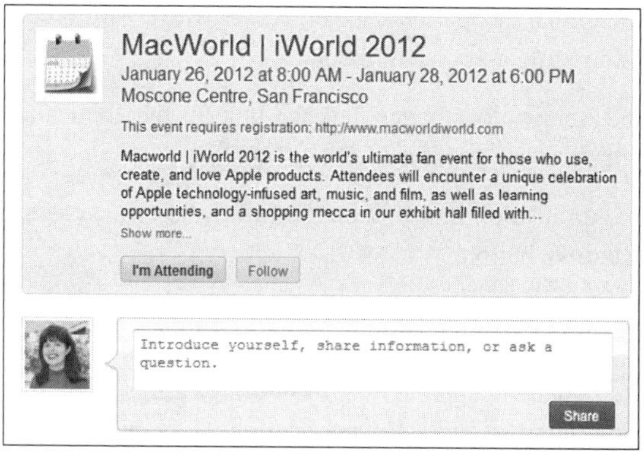

FIGURE 13.11   Use LinkedIn Events to find events to attend and share with your network.

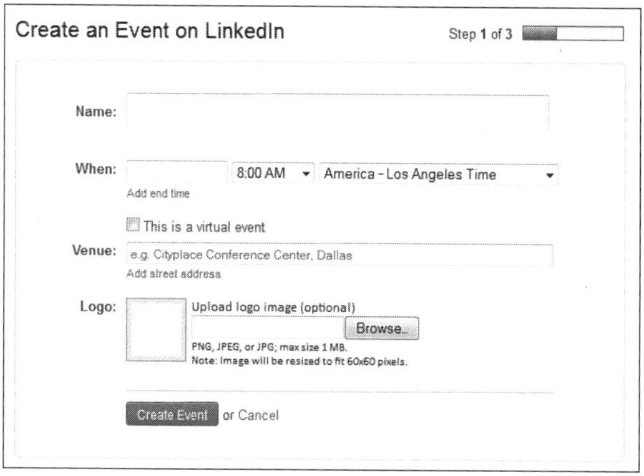

FIGURE 13.12   Create an event and publicize it on LinkedIn.

Removing Applications

Eventually, you might discover that an application isn't as useful as you thought it would be and you want to remove it:

1. On the global navigation bar, select **Get More Applications** from the More drop-down menu.

2. On the Applications page, click the link for the application you want to remove.

3. In the Application Info box on the right side of the page, click the **Remove** button.

LinkedIn removes the application from your profile and home page.

You can also update an application's visibility settings from this page. For example, rather than removing an application, you could choose not to display it on your profile or LinkedIn home page.

Summary

In this lesson, you learned how to use LinkedIn applications to enhance your profile and collaborate with your connections. Next, learn how to create a LinkedIn Company Page for your business.

LESSON 14

Working with Company Pages

In this lesson, you learn how to search for companies that meet your target criteria and create a LinkedIn Company Page for your own company.

Understanding LinkedIn Company Pages

LinkedIn Company Pages provide an opportunity for companies to present their products, services, and job openings to LinkedIn's vast audience. In addition, pages offer extensive data that's particularly useful to job seekers, recruiters, and members searching for potential clients and partners.

TIP: **Promote Your Small Business with a Company Page**

Company Pages aren't just for large corporations. If you own a small business, even a one-person business, creating a page can help you gain visibility on LinkedIn.

CAUTION: **Company Pages Aren't Advertisements**

Remember, however, that a Company Page isn't an advertisement in disguise. Stick to the facts and avoid hype. Read other pages in your industry before creating your own to understand what is and isn't appropriate.

Figure 14.1 shows a sample Company Page.

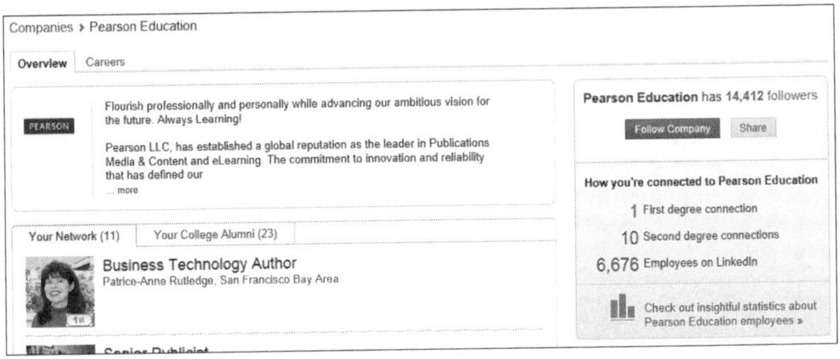

FIGURE 14.1   Learn more about a company on its Company Page.

Company Pages can include the following:

▶ A company summary

▶ A list of specialties

▶ Status updates from the company

▶ A Follow Company button that enables you to follow a company's activity on LinkedIn

▶ A Share button to share information about this company with other LinkedIn members

▶ Information about the company's products and services

▶ A list of current employees who are in your network or are alumni of the schools you attended

▶ A list of former employees in your network

▶ News about new hires and recent promotions

▶ Key statistics including top locations, company size, website link, common job titles, and median age of employees

▶ Links to open jobs posted on LinkedIn, if any

▶ Links to company news

▶ Stock information

The company icon to the right of any company name in a member profile indicates that the company has a LinkedIn Company Page. Click the company icon to view the page or hover over it to open a preview. Figure 14.2 shows a sample preview.

FIGURE 14.2   Preview a Company Page from a member profile.

NOTE: **What If the Company Icon Is Missing?**
If a company doesn't have a link or a company icon, no Company Page exists yet.

Searching for Companies

There are several ways to search for companies on LinkedIn.

Searching for Companies by Name

If you know the name of the company you want to find, follow these steps:

1. On the global navigation bar, select **Companies** from the drop-down list in the quick search box.

2. Enter the company name in the text box. As you type, LinkedIn displays potential matches in a drop-down list.

3. Select a company from the list to open its Company Page.

Searching for Companies by Specific Criteria

A quick search works well if you know the company you want to find. At times, however, you might want to search for companies that fit target criteria rather than locate a company you already know. For example, you can search for companies by keyword, industry, location, and so forth.

To search for companies based on criteria you specify, follow these steps:

1. On the global navigation bar, click the **Companies** link.

2. Select the **Search Companies** tab to open the Search Companies page.

3. If you want to search by keyword, enter your keywords in the text box above the Refine By box and click the **Search** button.

4. If you want to search for companies based on other criteria, specify that criteria in the Refine By box (see Figure 14.3). Your options include:

   ▶ **Location**—Search for companies based on location. If you only want to find companies with headquarters in this location, select the Headquarters Only check box.

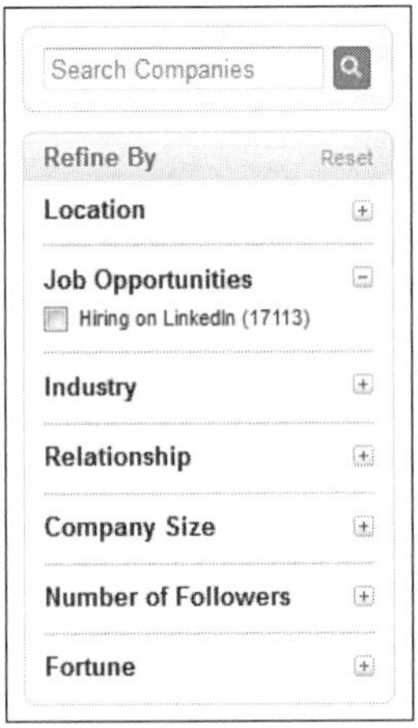

FIGURE 14.3   Specify the exact criteria of the companies you want to find.

▶ **Job Opportunities**—Search for companies that have job opportunities listed on LinkedIn.

▶ **Industry**—Search for companies in a specific industry.

▶ **Relationship**—Search for companies with employees in your network.

▶ **Company Size**—Search for companies with a specific number of employees.

▶ **Number of Followers**—Search for companies with a specific number of followers.

▶ **Fortune**—Search for companies on one of Fortune's lists.

As you select check boxes in the Refine By box, LinkedIn automatically filters the results that display on the right side of the page, as shown in Figure 14.4.

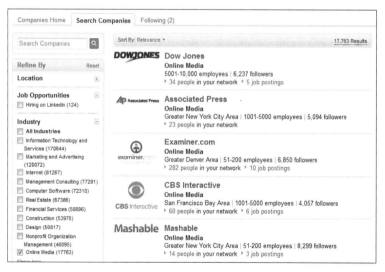

FIGURE 14.4   LinkedIn displays details about the companies that match your criteria.

Click a company's name to view its page. Refer to "Understanding LinkedIn Company Pages," earlier in this lesson, to learn more about the information available on a Company Page.

> TIP: **Specify Only the Most Pertinent Criteria**
> You don't need to complete all the fields in the Refine By box page to perform a search. In fact, you'll generate the best results by starting with your most important criteria and then modifying your criteria only if your initial search doesn't yield the desired results.

Creating a Company Page

If your company doesn't already have a Company Page, you can create one. Be aware that you must have the authority to create a page on behalf of a company (an important consideration if you work for a large organization). Creating a Company Page is a particularly good option for small businesses or solopreneurs seeking to promote their businesses on LinkedIn.

To create a page for your company, follow these steps:

1. Click the **Companies** link on the global navigation bar.

2. Click the **Add a Company** link at the top of the Companies page. The Add a Company page opens, shown in Figure 14.5.

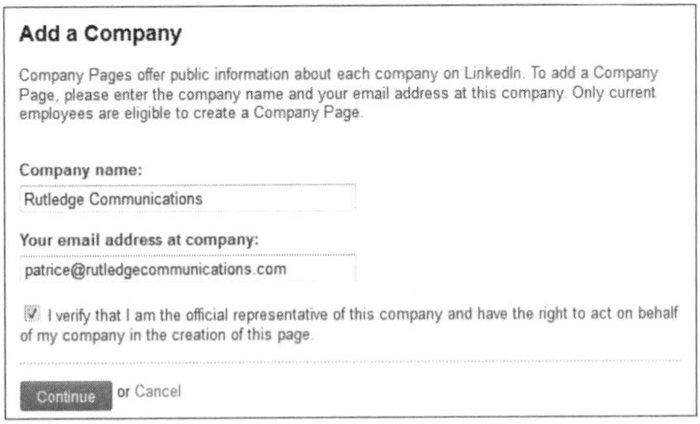

Add a Company

Company Pages offer public information about each company on LinkedIn. To add a Company Page, please enter the company name and your email address at this company. Only current employees are eligible to create a Company Page.

Company name:

Rutledge Communications

Your email address at company:

patrice@rutledgecommunications.com

☑ I verify that I am the official representative of this company and have the right to act on behalf of my company in the creation of this page.

Continue or Cancel

FIGURE 14.5   Creating a Company Page gives your company added visibility.

3. Enter your company name and email address and select the check box to verify that you have the right to create this page. You must enter an email address with a domain name for that company, not a web mail address such as Gmail or Yahoo! Mail.

4. Click the **Continue** button. LinkedIn prompts you to view the email confirmation sent to the email address you entered in step 3. You must verify your identity and your company before LinkedIn allows you to finish your page.

5. Follow the instructions in the email to confirm your email address. After doing so, LinkedIn takes you to the Confirm Your Email Address page.

6. On the Confirm Your Email Address page, click the **Confirm** button and sign in to LinkedIn again.

7. The Overview tab for your Company Page opens (see Figure 14.6), prompting you to add basic information for your company.

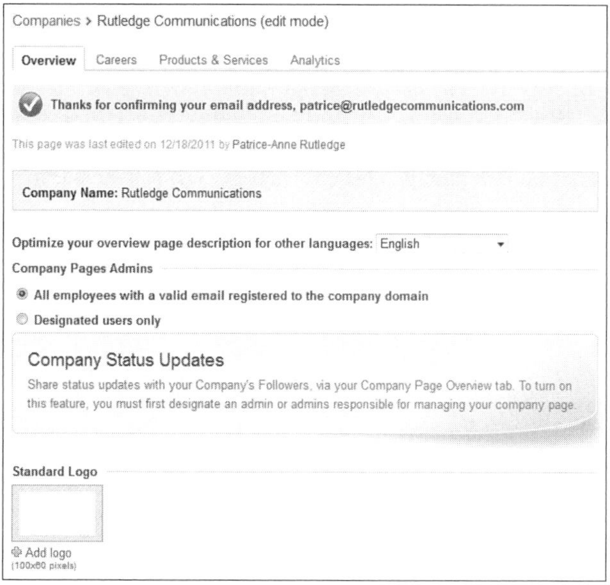

Companies > Rutledge Communications (edit mode)

Overview   Careers   Products & Services   Analytics

✓ Thanks for confirming your email address, patrice@rutledgecommunications.com

This page was last edited on 12/18/2011 by Patrice-Anne Rutledge

Company Name: Rutledge Communications

Optimize your overview page description for other languages: English ▾

Company Pages Admins

◉ All employees with a valid email registered to the company domain
○ Designated users only

Company Status Updates

Share status updates with your Company's Followers, via your Company Page Overview tab. To turn on this feature, you must first designate an admin or admins responsible for managing your company page.

Standard Logo

⊕ Add logo
(100x60 pixels)

FIGURE 14.6   Enter information about your company, including a detailed description.

8. Specify your page admins by choosing one of the following option buttons: **All Employees with a Valid Email Registered to the Company Domain** or **Designated Users Only**. In general, it's best to designate page admins because this offers the most security for your page. In addition, these designated users can post status updates to your page, which increases its visibility on LinkedIn.

9. Click the **Add Logo** button to select a logo. You can upload both a standard logo (100 × 60 pixels) for your page and a square logo (50 × 50 pixels) for display next to network updates. Logos must be in PNG, JPEG, or GIF format and no more than 100KB in size.

10. Add more details to your page by completing the remaining fields on the Overview tab. Be aware that fields preceded by a red asterisk are required fields. Options include Company Description, Company Specialties, Company Blog RSS Feed, and so on.

11. Optionally, click the **Products & Services** tab if you want to add information about your company's products and services (see Figure 14.7). This is a great promotional tool for most companies. For each item you list on this page, you can include a detailed description, image, YouTube video, special promotion, and link for more information.

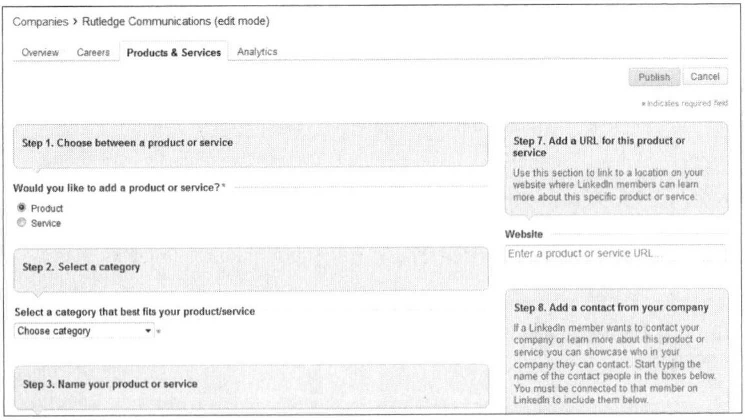

Companies > Rutledge Communications (edit mode)

Overview Careers **Products & Services** Analytics

Publish   Cancel

* Indicates required field

Step 1. Choose between a product or service

Would you like to add a product or service? *
⦿ Product
⦾ Service

Step 2. Select a category

Select a category that best fits your product/service
Choose category ▾ *

Step 3. Name your product or service

Step 7. Add a URL for this product or service

Use this section to link to a location on your website where LinkedIn members can learn more about this specific product or service.

Website
Enter a product or service URL...

Step 8. Add a contact from your company

If a LinkedIn member wants to contact your company or learn more about this product or service you can showcase who in your company they can contact. Start typing the name of the contact people in the boxes below. You must be connected to that member on LinkedIn to include them below.

FIGURE 14.7   Use the Products & Services tab to promote what your company has to offer.

> NOTE: **A Company Page Includes Two Other Tabs**
>
> A Company Page also includes two other tabs: Careers, which displays jobs you've posted on LinkedIn, and Analytics, which displays statistics about your page activity, such as page views, visitors, and clicks. Only page admins can view information about your page activity.

12. Click the **Publish** button to save changes and publish your Company Page.

Editing a Company Page

You can edit a Company Page that you created or that a Company Page Admin has authorized you to edit. When working in edit mode, you can modify your page's contents and view detailed analytics about your page.

To edit a Company Page, follow these steps:

1. On the global navigation bar, select your company from the **Companies** drop-down menu.

2. Select **Edit** from the Admin Tools drop-down button in the upper-right corner of the page (see Figure 14.8).

FIGURE 14.8   Edit your page any time you need to make updates.

3. Make your changes and click the **Publish** button to update and save your Company Page.

See "Creating a Company Page" section earlier in this lesson for more information about the data you can enter for a company.

Deleting a Company Page

If you no longer need your Company Page, you can delete it. For example, you might want to delete your page if you close your business.

To delete a Company Page, follow these steps:

1. On the global navigation bar, select your company from the **Companies** drop-down menu.

2. Select **Delete** from the Admin Tools drop-down button in the upper-right corner of the page.

3. In the Please Confirm dialog box, click the **Yes, Please Delete It** button to confirm deletion. Be aware that you can't undo a deletion.

Associating Employees with a Company Page

LinkedIn associates employees automatically with the pages of the employers that they list on their profiles. If LinkedIn doesn't list you correctly as an employee of your company, follow these steps to edit your company information:

1. On the global navigation bar, select **Edit Profile** from the Profile drop-down menu. The Edit Profile page opens.

2. Click the **Edit** link next to your current position. The Edit Position page opens.

3. Click the **Change Company** link and enter a new company name. When you start typing, LinkedIn suggests possible matches. Be careful to choose the correct match. With larger companies in particular, you might find subsidiaries, divisions, or even incorrect spellings.

4. Click the **Update** button to update your profile.

> NOTE: **Removing Employees from Your Company Page**
>
> If LinkedIn members incorrectly identify themselves as employees of your company, contact LinkedIn's Customer Service to have them removed.

Summary

In this lesson, you learned how to search for companies that meet targeted criteria, create your own Company Page for exposure on LinkedIn's network, and update existing pages. Next, learn how to access LinkedIn Mobile when you're on the go.

Using LinkedIn Mobile

Learn how to keep up with LinkedIn using your mobile phone.

Using LinkedIn Mobile

LinkedIn Mobile enables you to view selected LinkedIn data and perform selected LinkedIn tasks on your mobile phone. If you use a BlackBerry, iPhone, Android smartphone, or Palm device, you should also consider the LinkedIn application specific to your phone.

To learn more about LinkedIn Mobile options, click the **Mobile** link on the bottom navigation menu.

Accessing LinkedIn on Your Mobile Phone

With LinkedIn Mobile, you can access LinkedIn on any mobile phone with Internet access.

To access LinkedIn on your mobile phone, follow these steps:

1. Point to http://touch.linkedin.com.

2. Enter your email address and LinkedIn password.

3. Click the **Sign In** button.

Using the LinkedIn iPhone Application

LinkedIn offers a free application for the iPhone that's compatible with the iPod touch and iPad and integrates with your iPhone address book. This application requires iOS 4.0 or later. It's available in English, Chinese, French, German, Italian, Japanese, Portuguese, and Spanish.

Figure 15.1 shows network updates on the iPhone.

FIGURE 15.1   View LinkedIn network updates on your iPhone.

To download this application, click the **Mobile** link on the bottom navigation menu and then click the **iPhone** link on the LinkedIn Mobile page. Alternatively, search the App Store in iTunes.

Using the LinkedIn for Android Application

The LinkedIn for Android application enables you to access LinkedIn from any Android device that uses Android 2.1 and up.

Figure 15.2 shows network updates on the Android.

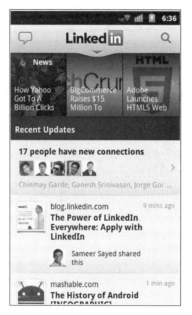

FIGURE 15.2   Access LinkedIn on the go with your Android device.

To download LinkedIn for Android, click the **Mobile** link on the bottom navigation menu and then click the **Android** link on the LinkedIn Mobile page. Alternatively, search Android Market (https://market.android.com).

Using LinkedIn on Your BlackBerry

LinkedIn for BlackBerry enables you to work with your BlackBerry contacts, calendar, and messaging. This application is available for Tour, Bold, Curve, Storm, and Pearl using OS 4.3.0 or higher.

To download LinkedIn for BlackBerry, click the **Mobile** link on the bottom navigation menu and then click the **BlackBerry** link on the LinkedIn Mobile page. Alternatively, type the following link on your BlackBerry: http://m.linkedin.com/blackberry/download.

Using LinkedIn on Your Palm

If you own a Palm Pre or Palm Pixi, you can download the free LinkedIn application in the Palm application catalog. This app enables you to search and view profiles, send email to your connections, send invitations to connect, and view and accept outstanding invitations.

To download, click the **Mobile** link on the bottom navigation menu and then click the **Palm** link on the LinkedIn Mobile page.

Summary

In this lesson, you learned how to access LinkedIn from your mobile phone and download device-specific LinkedIn mobile applications. Next, learn how to recruit the best job candidates on LinkedIn.

Recruiting Job Candidates

In this lesson, you learn about LinkedIn's many options for recruiting top talent.

Understanding LinkedIn's Recruitment Options

Even in an employer's market, it can be difficult to find the right candidate, particularly for a job that requires specific expertise and experience. Fortunately, LinkedIn offers numerous options for recruiters, hiring managers, and small businesses to locate and recruit top talent.

On LinkedIn, you can:

▶ Pay to post a 30-day job listing that's searchable by LinkedIn's millions of members (the exact price varies based on geographic location)

▶ Purchase job credits for discounted job postings

▶ Post a job on a group's Jobs Discussion Board at no cost

▶ Search for candidates using LinkedIn's advanced search features

▶ Perform reference searches on potential candidates

▶ Upgrade to a premium account to send more InMails to potential candidates

▶ Sign up for LinkedIn Corporate Recruiting Solutions, a comprehensive set of recruitment tools for larger companies

Which option is right for you depends on your budget, the size of your company, and the type of candidates you want to attract.

Posting a Job

LinkedIn charges a fixed fee for a 30-day job posting. The exact fee varies based on geographic location. If you plan to post multiple jobs, you can save money by purchasing discount job credits. See the "Purchasing Job Credits" section later in this lesson for more information.

To post a job on LinkedIn, follow these steps:

1. On the global navigation bar, select **Post a Job** from the Jobs drop-down menu. The Step 1—Create Your Job page opens, shown in Figure 16.1.

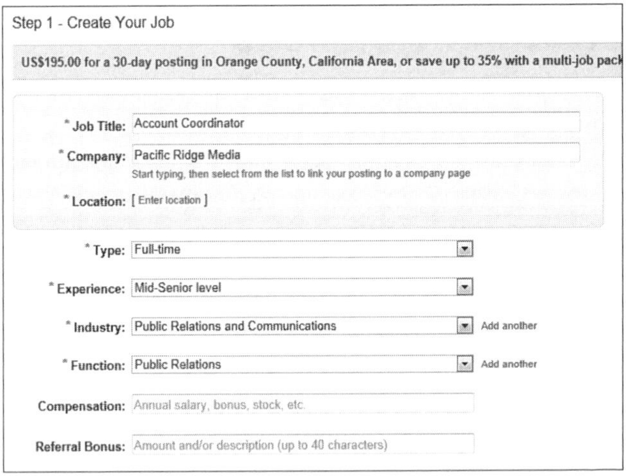

FIGURE 16.1   Post a job that could reach millions of LinkedIn members.

TIP: **Create a Detailed Job Posting for Better Results**

The Step 1—Create Your Job page lists several fields as optional, but you'll get better results with a job posting that contains as much detail as possible. In addition to basic job duties, emphasize the perks and benefits of the position to attract quality candidates.

2. Enter a job title and verify that the text box to the right of this field displays the correct company name. The job poster's current company appears by default, but you can edit this text box.

3. Click the **Enter Location** link to open the Job Price Calculator dialog box, shown in Figure 16.2.

FIGURE 16.2   Enter a postal code to learn how much your job posting will cost.

4. Enter the postal code for this job's location to display the price for your job posting. Pricing varies by location.

5. Select the **30-Day Posting** option button. If you want to post more than one job, see "Purchasing Job Credits" later in this lesson to learn about job packs.

6. Click the **Continue** button to close the Job Price Calculator dialog box and return to the Create Your Job page.

7. Enter an optional location description. This is particularly useful for pinpointing the exact city the job is located in or the specific neighborhood for larger cities (such as midtown Manhattan).

8. In the Type drop-down list, select one of the following: Full-time, Part-time, Contract, Temporary, or Other.

9. Indicate the experience level of your desired candidate, such as executive, director, mid-senior level, associate, entry level, internship, or not applicable.

10. Select an industry and job function for your job. To add another industry or function, click the **Add Another** link. You can include up to three industries and three job functions per job.

11. Enter optional compensation information such as base salary, bonus potential, and so forth.

12. Enter optional referral bonus information of up to 40 characters.

13. Enter a detailed job description of up to 25,000 characters. Candidates search for jobs using keywords. Be sure your post contains the right keywords to attract top candidates. Job skills, certifications, and degrees—such as Java, PMP, CPA, and MBA—are good keywords.

14. Provide optional information about the skills required and a company description. You can enter up to 4,000 characters in each text box. The Company Description box pulls existing content from your LinkedIn Company Page if you have one.

CAUTION: **Proofread Your Posting Carefully**

Before posting your job, check it carefully for spelling, grammar, and content errors.

---

15. In the Applicant Routing section, specify how you want to receive applications. Your options include sending applications to an email address or directing applicants to an external website such as your company's own job listing page.

16. In the Job Poster section, indicate whether you want to display your profile on the job listing.

TIP: **Save Your Posting as a Draft**

If you want to save your In-progress job posting, click the **Save as Draft** button. To return to your saved draft, select **Manage Your Jobs** from the Jobs drop-down list on global navigation bar.

---

17. Click the **Continue** button. The Step 2—Profile Matches page opens, shown in Figure 16.3.

FIGURE 16.3   Specify whether you want LinkedIn to find candidate matches in step 2.

18. The Profile Matches page displays LinkedIn members who are potential matches for your job based on their profile content. To view the full profiles of the best matches and contact up to 10 of them via InMail, select the **Yes, I Wish to Unlock All Matches** check box at the bottom of the page. Be aware that LinkedIn will charge you an additional $95 for this service.

19. Click the **Continue** button to open the Billing Information page. Alternatively, click the **Go Back** button to return to the previous page.

20. Enter your billing information and credit card data (unless you have available job credits), and then click **Review Order** (see Figure 16.4) to review your order and finalize your job posting.

TIP: **Post a Job on a Group's Jobs Discussion Board**

Another option for posting jobs on LinkedIn is to post on a relevant group's Jobs Discussion Board. Although there is no cost to post on this board and you might attract targeted applicants, this type of posting doesn't offer the same level of visibility of a traditional job posting.

Your posted job appears on LinkedIn for 30 days. To manage your open jobs, select **Manage Your Jobs** from the Jobs drop-down menu on the global navigation bar. The Manage Jobs page opens, shown in Figure 16.5, where you can:

▶ Complete and post a draft job posting

▶ View open and closed (past) job postings

▶ Inform your network about your job postings

▶ Search for potential candidates

▶ Review job applicants' resumes and cover letters

▶ Perform reference searches

FIGURE 16.4   Enter your billing and credit card information before posting your job.

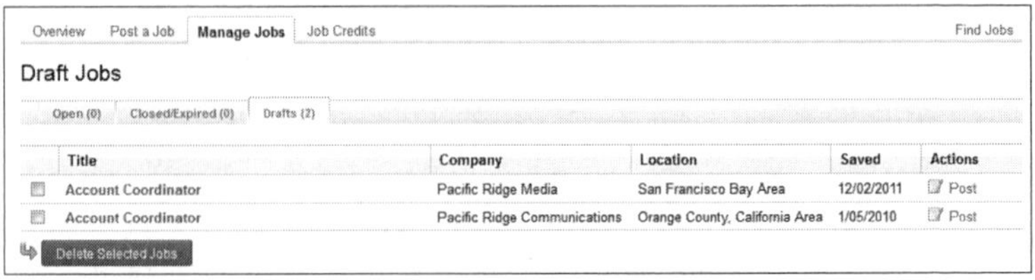

FIGURE 16.5   Manage drafts, open jobs, and closed (past) jobs on the Manage Jobs page.

Purchasing Job Credits

Purchasing job credits can save you money if you post jobs on LinkedIn frequently, yet don't want to upgrade to LinkedIn Corporate Recruiting Solutions. A *job credit* is a prepaid credit for posting a single job. Job credits come in packages of five or ten credits with discounts off the standard fee for a single, full-price job posting.

To purchase job credits, follow these steps:

   1. On the global navigation bar, select **Post a Job** from the Jobs drop-down menu.

   2. Click the **Enter Location** link to open the Job Price Calculator dialog box, shown in Figure 16.6.

FIGURE 16.6   Save money by purchasing LinkedIn job credits.

   3. Select your country from the drop-down list and enter a postal code, if applicable. Your location determines the cost of your job credits.

   4. Select the number of job credits you want to purchase. You can purchase either a 5-job pack or a 10-job pack. If you want to post a single job, see "Posting a Job" earlier in this lesson for more information.

5. Click the **Continue** button.

6. Enter your contact and credit card information on the Billing Information page.

7. Click the **Review Order** button to review your order and purchase your credits, which are available the next time you post a job.

To track your job credits, select **Manage Your Jobs** from the Job drop-down menu on the global navigation bar and select the **Job Credits** tab. Here you can view details about your active and used credits.

Searching for Job Candidates

At times, you might want to search for passive job candidates in addition to considering the candidates who apply directly for your open positions. Here are some search strategies for finding qualified passive candidates:

▶ View the people connecting to your connections who perform a similar job.

▶ Perform an advanced search for LinkedIn members who meet specific criteria. See Lesson 7, "Searching on LinkedIn," for more information.

▶ Search groups for members whose participation enhances the goals of the group. See Lesson 11, "Participating in LinkedIn Groups," for more information.

▶ Search LinkedIn Answers for members who provide intelligent answers to questions in your field. See Lesson 12, "Using LinkedIn Answers," for more information.

TIP: **Upgrade to Contact More Candidates by InMail**

If you plan to contact potential job or reference candidates by InMail, consider upgrading to a premium account that includes a specified number of InMails per month. For more information, click the **Upgrade My Account** link on the bottom navigation menu.

Performing Reference Searches

LinkedIn reference searches are a premium feature that let you search for LinkedIn members who worked at the same company at the same time as a candidate you're considering for a job.

To perform a reference search, follow these steps:

1. Select the **People** option on the quick search box that appears on the global navigation bar.

2. Click the **Advanced** link to the right of the search box. The Advanced People Search page opens.

3. Click the **Reference Search** tab, shown in Figure 16.7.

FIGURE 16.7   Perform reference searches on potential job candidates.

4. Enter the Company Name, Candidate, and Years of Employment in the text boxes.

5. Click the **Search** button. The Find References: Search Results page displays information about people in your network who meet the criteria you specified.

If you don't have a premium account and haven't posted a job, the returned results will show only the number of people who meet the criteria. To see more details, you need to have a premium account. Click the **Upgrade Now** button to view upgrade options.

LinkedIn offers two other ways to search for similar reference information at no cost. You can:

▶ Click the name of a company on a candidate's profile and view the list of current and former employees on the company profile.

▶ Perform an advanced people search, specifying the candidate's company and location. Refer to Lesson 7 for more information on advanced searches.

If you're a premium member or if you paid for a job posting, you can click the **Find References** link on a member's profile or next to a specific applicant on the Manage Jobs page.

Using LinkedIn Corporate Recruiting Solutions

LinkedIn Corporate Recruiting Solutions offers a comprehensive set of recruitment tools for major companies.

LinkedIn Corporate Recruiting Solutions includes the following components:

▶ **LinkedIn Recruiter**—Enable a team of recruiters to collaborate, manage the recruitment process, source passive job candidates, and share multiple InMails per month.

▶ **Referral Engine**—Generate employee-driven candidate leads.

▶ **Jobs Network**—Post jobs with precision targeting, candidate match recommendation, and viral distribution.

▶ **Jobs for You**—Display personalized jobs on the Web that target a specific audience.

▶ **Talent Direct**—Create targeted direct InMail campaigns.

▶ **Career Pages**—Publish a Career Page for your company with custom content, including employee spotlights and video.

▶ **Work with Us**—Place job ads on your employees' LinkedIn profiles.

▶ **Recruitment Ads**—Position your company as an employer of choice through targeted ads.

▶ **Recruitment Insights**—Use surveys to improve your online recruitment.

To learn more, click the **Recruiting Solutions** link on the bottom navigation menu.

Summary

In this lesson, you learned about LinkedIn's many recruiting options, including job postings, job credits, candidate and reference searches, and LinkedIn Corporate Recruiting Solutions. Next, learn how to create and manage an advertising campaign using LinkedIn Ads.

LESSON 17

Advertising on LinkedIn

In this lesson, you learn about LinkedIn advertising programs. You also learn how to create and manage an advertising campaign using LinkedIn Ads.

Understanding LinkedIn Ads

LinkedIn Ads offers a text-based advertising program that focuses on reaching the site's highly targeted demographics with ads placed on the home page and member profiles.

LinkedIn Ads enables businesses with advertising budgets as low as $10 per day to display text ads on LinkedIn. The LinkedIn Ads program is a self-service advertising option, similar to Google AdWords. You enter your ad online and pay for it with a credit card.

Ads on LinkedIn display in different formats depending on where they are placed on the site. Figure 17.1 shows a sample text ad at the top of the home page. Figure 17.2 shows a sample ad with a logo.

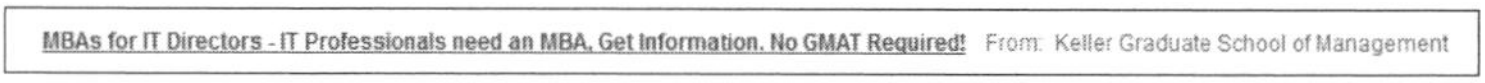

MBAs for IT Directors - IT Professionals need an MBA. Get Information. No GMAT Required!
From: Keller Graduate School of Management

FIGURE 17.1 You can create your own text ads to advertise to specific LinkedIn members.

esi
Numeric Hydrogeologist
Vacancy for a qualified quantitative hydrogeologist with 3years+ experience
www.esinternational.com
From: Cliff Walcott

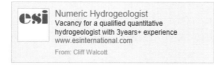

FIGURE 17.2 Sample LinkedIn ad with logo.

Creating a LinkedIn Ad

It takes only a few minutes to set up an ad, but it's a good idea to spend a bit more time analyzing your approach, content, and goals if you want to succeed. Here are some tips for creating ads that generate results:

▸ **Because a text ad contains so few words, make every word count**—Your first effort will most likely contain too many words. Keep revising until you can communicate your message effectively within the ad length limitations.

▸ **Focus on a call to action**—You need to pique the interest of your target audience and encourage them to click your ad for more information.

▸ **Check your grammar and spelling**—Errors make your ad look unprofessional and reduce your click-through rate.

▸ **Verify that your URL works**—Even worse than grammar and spelling errors is a URL that doesn't work or leads to the wrong place.

▸ **Avoid using all capitalization in your ad**—Use title case for your headline and sentence case for your remaining ad.

▸ **Avoid ad content and topics that violate LinkedIn Ads Guidelines**—This includes ads for alcohol, tobacco, drugs, gambling, firearms, adult products, dating services, or multi-level marketing programs. Click the **Advertising Guidelines** link at the bottom of any LinkedIn Ads page to view the complete guidelines.

To place a LinkedIn ad, follow these steps:

1. On the bottom navigation menu, click the **Advertising** link to access LinkedIn Ads.

2. Click the **Start Now** button to open the Create Ad Campaign page, shown in Figure 17.3.

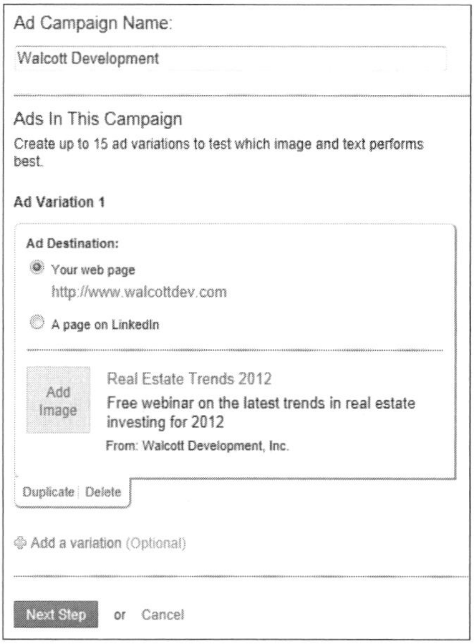

FIGURE 17.3   Write and preview your LinkedIn ad.

3. In the Ad Campaign Name box, enter a descriptive name for your ad. This doesn't appear on your ad; it's for your reference only.

4. Select an ad destination, either a web page or a page on LinkedIn, such as your LinkedIn Company Page.

5. Click the **Add Image** link to open the Upload Your Logo dialog box where you can select an image to display on your ad. Logos must be in PNG, JPEG, or GIF format and no more than 2MB in size. Images display only on ads in locations that support an ad thumbnail.

6. Enter a headline of up to 25 characters. Your headline is what draws members to your ad. Make it memorable and clear.

7. Enter your ad text of up to 75 characters, which can span two lines.

8. Select your **Profile Link** from the drop-down list. You can display either your personal LinkedIn profile or a LinkedIn Company Page.

> CAUTION: **Your Profile Link Is Mandatory**
>
> You can't remove your profile link from your ad; it's mandatory. LinkedIn doesn't allow anonymous ads.

9. If you want to create multiple variations of your ads, click the **Add a Variation** link and complete the new ad. For example, you could change the headline or wording slightly to see which ad performs better. To save time, click the **Duplicate** link in your first ad to duplicate and then modify it. You can create up to 15 ad variations.

10. Click the **Next Step** button to open the Targeting page (see Figure 17.4).

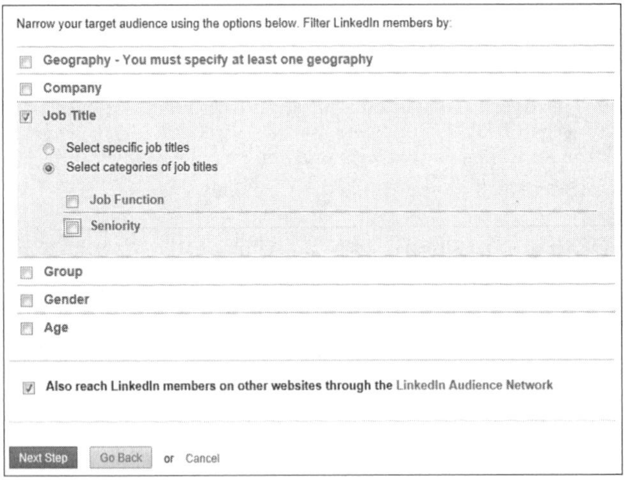

Narrow your target audience using the options below. Filter LinkedIn members by:

☐ Geography - You must specify at least one geography

☐ Company

☑ Job Title

   ◯ Select specific job titles
   ◉ Select categories of job titles

      ☐ Job Function
      ☐ Seniority

☐ Group

☐ Gender

☐ Age

☑ Also reach LinkedIn members on other websites through the LinkedIn Audience Network

[Next Step] [Go Back]   or   Cancel

FIGURE 17.4   Accurate targeting helps create a more successful ad.

11. Select the check boxes for the filters you want to apply. These include:

- ► **Geography**—Select up to 10 geographic areas. In many locations, you can narrow your target audience to a specific metro area. You must select at least one geographic location for your ad.

- ► **Company**—Enter companies by name or select from a variety of industries.

- ► **Job Title**—Enter specific job titles or select categories of job titles based on job function or seniority.

- ► **Group**—Enter the name of a LinkedIn group to target members of that group. As you type, LinkedIn displays potential matches for you to choose.

- ► **Gender**—Select a gender (if your ad targets either a male or female audience).

- ► **Age**—Select the age ranges you want to target.

12. View the Estimated Target Audience field to see the effects of narrowing your audience. You can modify your criteria if the summary results don't match the audience size you want to reach.

TIP: **Analyze Your Target Audience Carefully**

Before continuing to the next page, review your estimated target audience carefully. Consider who you want to reach and why. Is your estimated target audience too big or too small? Sometimes a small target audience can yield better results, but other times it just doesn't give you enough reach.

---

13. If you want to display your ad on LinkedIn partner sites as well as LinkedIn.com, select the **Also Reach LinkedIn Members on Other Websites Through the LinkedIn Audience Network** check box.

14. Click the **Next Step** button to open the Campaign Options page, shown in Figure 17.5.

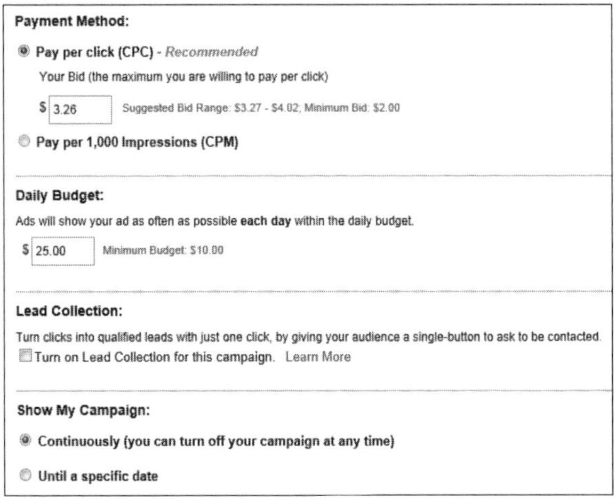

Payment Method:

◉ Pay per click (CPC) - *Recommended*

Your Bid (the maximum you are willing to pay per click)

$ 3.26   Suggested Bid Range: $3.27 - $4.02; Minimum Bid: $2.00

○ Pay per 1,000 Impressions (CPM)

Daily Budget:

Ads will show your ad as often as possible **each day** within the daily budget.

$ 25.00   Minimum Budget: $10.00

Lead Collection:

Turn clicks into qualified leads with just one click, by giving your audience a single-button to ask to be contacted.

☐ Turn on Lead Collection for this campaign. Learn More

Show My Campaign:

◉ Continuously (you can turn off your campaign at any time)

○ Until a specific date

FIGURE 17.5   Establish your budget and select a pricing model.

15. Select the **Pay per Click (CPC)** option button if you want to pay based on the number of times a LinkedIn member clicks your ad. Enter the maximum amount you're willing to pay for each click. You might pay less per click depending on demand, but you won't pay more than this amount. LinkedIn displays a suggested range based on the current bids of other advertisers, but you can enter any amount you want that meets or exceeds the minimum of $2.

> PLAIN ENGLISH: **CPC**
>
> *CPC* is a common online advertising term that stands for *cost per click*. When you choose a CPC advertising model, you pay only when someone clicks your ad.

16. Select the **Pay per 1,000 Impressions (CPM)** option button if you want to pay for every 1,000 impressions your ad receives. Enter the maximum amount you're willing to pay for each of the 1,000 impressions. You might pay less depending on demand, but you won't pay more than this amount. LinkedIn displays a suggested range based on the current bids of other advertisers, but you can enter any amount you want that meets or exceeds the minimum of $2.

PLAIN ENGLISH: CPM

CPM is a common online advertising term that stands for *cost per thousand* views. When you choose a CPM advertising model, you pay a fixed amount for every 1,000 ad views regardless of how many clicks it receives.

---

17. Enter the amount of money you're willing to spend each day in the Daily Budget field. LinkedIn continues to display your ad until you reach this limit. The minimum you can enter is $10.

18. Select the **Lead Collection** check box if you want to display a button that people can click to request contact. Click the **Learn More** link for more information about lead collection.

19. Specify whether you want to show your campaign continuously or until a specified date. It's best to run a long-term campaign unless you're marketing something that's time-sensitive, such as an event.

20. Click the **Next Step** button to open the Billing Information page.

21. Enter your personal and credit card information in the specified fields.

22. Click the **Review Order** button to review your order and place your ad. LinkedIn charges your credit card $5 and credits this amount to your LinkedIn Ads account.

LinkedIn reviews your ad to verify that it meets its advertising guidelines. Until your ad is approved, its status is *Under Review*.

Managing Your LinkedIn Ads

After receiving approval from LinkedIn, your ad will begin to appear on the LinkedIn site based on the targeted criteria you specify.

To manage your ads and view reports of your results, go to https://www.linkedin.com/ads/home.

This page has four tabs:

▶ **Ad Campaigns**—View a summary of your results for each ad, such as your status, daily budget, ad clicks, impressions, click-through rate (CTR), average cost-per-click (CPC), and total spent. You can also click an ad name for more details, turn your ads on and off the LinkedIn network, and hide them from this tab.

▶ **Leads**—View a list of your leads, which you can filter by date, contact status, and campaign.

▶ **Reporting**—View reports that detail your impressions and clicks over specific time periods (see Figure 17.6). You can download the reports in a CSV (comma-separated values) format to import into applications such as Microsoft Excel.

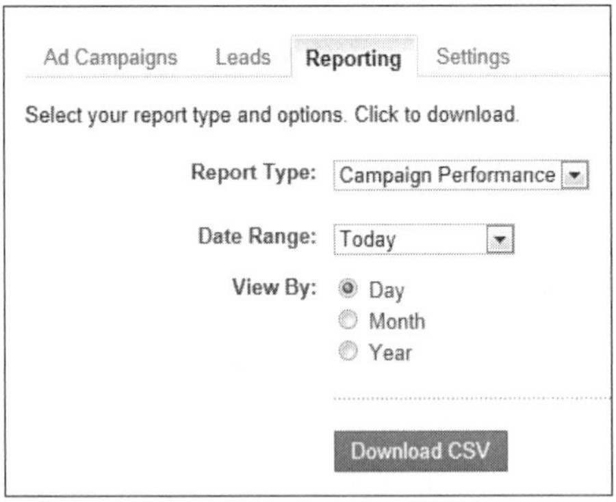

FIGURE 17.6   Analyze your reporting data and adjust your LinkedIn Ads campaign if necessary.

▶ **Settings**—Give permission to LinkedIn to contact you about ad problems, campaigns that are ending, or campaign optimization opportunities.

PLAIN ENGLISH: **CTR**

CTR is a common online advertising term that stands for *click-through rate*. Your CTR tells you the percentage of people who clicked your ad. Remember, however, that some people don't immediately click links in ads; they do, however, later visit website links that are shown in ads.

TIP: **Create a Business Account to Manage Your LinkedIn Ads**

If you would rather manage your ads from a business account than your personal LinkedIn account, click the down arrow next to your name in the upper-right corner of the screen and select **Create Business Account** from the menu that displays.

Summary

In this lesson, you learned about LinkedIn advertising programs and how to create and manage a LinkedIn Ads campaign.

Index

B

Basic Information page (profiles), 21-22

basic profile information, entering, 21-22

benefits of LinkedIn, 3-4

Billing Information page, 215

Blackberry app, 210

Blog Link application, 182-184

Bookmark link (Jobs page), 126

Box.net Files application, 184-185

Browse Open Questions page, 171-173

browser toolbars, 107

    LinkedIn Firefox Browser Toolbar, 108-109

    LinkedIn Internet Explorer Toolbar, 110-111

browsing questions to answer, 171-173

business accounts, creating, 231

business partner recommendations, 133

buttons. *See specific buttons*

C

Campaign Options page, 228

candidates, searching for, 218

Change Contact Preferences link (Edit Profile page), 36

changing

    Company Pages, 203

    display order of groups, 158-159

    email address, 56, 66

    passwords, 57, 66

    profile photo, 64

    questions and answers, 177-178

    recommendations, 145

Choose File to Upload dialog box, 44

choosing applications, 180-181

classmates, connecting with, 46

click-through rate (CTR), 231

Close Question Now button, 177

closing accounts, 66

colleagues

    colleague recommendations, 133

    connecting with, 45-46

Colleagues page, 45-46

comma-separated values files (.CSV), 43

Comment button, 152

comments

    adding to group discussions, 152

    on profile updates, 73

companies

    searching

        by criteria, 198-200

        by name, 197

    settings, 62-63

Company Pages

    associating employees with, 204-205

    creating, 200-203

    deleting, 204

    editing, 203

    explained, 195-197

    searching for companies

        by criteria, 198-200

        by name, 197

M

S

Sams**TeachYourself**

from Sams Publishing

Sams **Teach Yourself in 10 Minutes** offers straightforward, practical answers for fast results.

These small books of 250 pages or less offer tips that point out shortcuts and solutions, cautions that help you avoid common pitfalls, and notes that explain additional concepts and provide additional information. By working through the 10-minute lessons, you learn everything you need to know quickly and easily!

When you only have time for the answers, Sams Teach Yourself books are your best solution.

Visit **informit.com/samsteachyourself** for a complete listing of the products available.

SAMS

REGISTER

THIS PRODUCT

informit.com/register

Register the Addison-Wesley, Exam Cram, Prentice Hall, Que, and Sams products you own to unlock great benefits.

To begin the registration process, simply go to **informit.com/register** to sign in or create an account. You will then be prompted to enter the 10- or 13-digit ISBN that appears on the back cover of your product.

Registering your products can unlock the following benefits:
- Access to supplemental content, including bonus chapters, source code, or project files.
- A coupon to be used on your next purchase.

Registration benefits vary by product. Benefits will be listed on your Account page under Registered Products.

About InformIT — THE TRUSTED TECHNOLOGY LEARNING SOURCE

INFORMIT IS HOME TO THE LEADING TECHNOLOGY PUBLISHING IMPRINTS Addison-Wesley Professional, Cisco Press, Exam Cram, IBM Press, Prentice Hall Professional, Que, and Sams. Here you will gain access to quality and trusted content and resources from the authors, creators, innovators, and leaders of technology. Whether you're looking for a book on a new technology, a helpful article, timely newsletters, or access to the Safari Books Online digital library, InformIT has a solution for you.

THE TRUSTED TECHNOLOGY LEARNING SOURCE

Addison-Wesley | Cisco Press | Exam Cram
IBM Press | Que | Prentice Hall | Sams

SAFARI BOOKS ONLINE

Sams Teach Yourself

LinkedIn
in 10 Minutes

SAMS

Patrice-Anne Rutledge

Third Edition

Safari
Books Online

FREE
Online Edition

Your purchase of *Sams Teach Yourself LinkedIn® in 10 Minutes* includes access to a free online edition for 45 days through the **Safari Books Online** subscription service. Nearly every Sams book is available online through **Safari Books Online**, along with thousands of books and videos from publishers such as Addison-Wesley Professional, Cisco Press, Exam Cram, IBM Press, O'Reilly Media, Prentice Hall, Que, and VMware Press.

Safari Books Online is a digital library providing searchable, on-demand access to thousands of technology, digital media, and professional development books and videos from leading publishers. With one monthly or yearly subscription price, you get unlimited access to learning tools and information on topics including mobile app and software development, tips and tricks on using your favorite gadgets, networking, project management, graphic design, and much more

Activate your FREE Online Edition at
informit.com/safarifree

STEP 1:   Enter the coupon code: TQQWEBI.

STEP 2:   New Safari users, complete the brief registration form.
Safari subscribers, just log in.

If you have difficulty registering on Safari or accessing the online edition,
please e-mail customer-service@safaribooksonline.com

AdobePress   ALPHA   Cisco Press   FT Press   IBM Press   Microsoft Press   New Riders   O'REILLY

Prentice Press   Prentice Hall   QUE   Redbooks   SAMS   SAS Publishing   vmware PRESS   WILEY   wrox